The Canadian Battlefields in Belgium, the Netherlands and Germany, 1944-1945

A Visitor's Guide

Terry Copp &
Mike Bechthold

Laurier Centre for Military Strategic and Disarmament Studies

Dedicated to the men and women
of the Canadian Forces who fought
for the liberation of Europe and
the hope of a better world.

First published in 2005 by the Laurier Centre for Military Strategic and Disarmament Studies, Wilfrid Laurier University, Waterloo, Ontario, Canada, (519)884-0710 x.4594, mbechthold@wlu.ca

National Library of Canada Cataloguing in Publication

Copp, Terry, 1938-

The Canadian battlefields in Belgium, the Netherlands and Germany, 1944-1945 : a visitor's guide / Terry Copp & Mike Bechthold.

Previously published under title: The Canadian battlefields in northwest Europe.
ISBN 978-1-926804-02-6

1. World War, 1939-1945—Battlefields—Europe, Western—Guidebooks. 2. World War, 1939-1945—Campaigns—Belgium. 3. World War, 1939-1945—Campaigns—Netherlands. 4. World War, 1939-1945—Campaigns—Germany. 5. Canada. Canadian Army—History—World War, 1939-1945. 6. Europe, Western—Guidebooks. I. Bechthold, Michael, 1968- II. Laurier Centre for Military, Strategic and Disarmament Studies III. Title.

D747.C65 2010 940.54'21 C2010-907638-9

MIX
Paper from responsible sources
FSC www.fsc.org FSC® C016245

Book and Cover Design: Mike Bechthold
Maps: Mike Bechthold
Photos (unless otherwise credited): Mike Bechthold
Printed and bound in Canada

Contents

The Strategic Debate in September 1944 7

Operation Market Garden 13

Belgium and the Breskens Pocket 17

Flanders 17

Operation "Switchback": The Breskens Pocket 22

The Tour 37

North From Antwerp: Woensdrecht, Walcheren, Bergen-op-Zoom 47

Woensdrecht 49

Beveland and Walcheren Island 57

Bergen-op-Zoom 61

The Tour 65

The Rhineland and the Rhine Crossing 75

The Tour 96

The Liberation of the Netherlands 103

3rd Division: Zutphen, Deventer and Leeuwarden 104

1st Division: The Ijssel Bridgehead and Apeldoorn 108

5th Division: Otterlo and Barneveld 114

2nd Division: The Advance to Groningen 117

4th Division: Delden, Sögel and the Küsten Canal 122

The Last Battles: Delfzijl, Leer, Bad Zwischenahn, Oldenburg and Wismar 125

The Tour 131

List of Maps

Battle Maps

Pursuit from the Seine, 26 August-12 September 1944 8
Montgomery's Narrow Front Strategy 12
Eisenhower's Broad Front Strategy 12
Operation Market Garden 15
British 1st Airborne Division at Arnhem 16
The Scheldt Estuary 22
The Breskens Pocket 24
Operation Switchback: The Leopold Canal 28
Operation Switchback: 9th Brigade Landings 33
North From Antwerp 49
Woensdrecht 51
Bergen-op-Zoom and vicinity 61
Walcheren, October-November 1944 67
Kapelsche Veer 72
Closing to the Rhine: 31 January to 24 March 1945 77
The Rhineland: Operation "Veritable" 78
Moyland Wood 80
The Rhineland: Operation "Blockbuster" 83
The Hochwald Gap 86
Operations Plunder and Varsity: 23-27 March 1945 89
Operation Plunder: 9th Canadian Infantry Brigade 93
Emmerich and the Rhine River 94
First Canadian Army in the Netherlands, 1945 107
Advance to Apeldoorn, 11-14 April 1945 108
The Battle for Apeldoorn: 14-17 April 1945 112
Otterlo, 16-17 April 1945 115
Western Holland: 2-25 April 1945 115
Groningen 118
The Northern Front: 27 March to 19 April 1945 124
The Emden Fortress 124
The Delfzijl Pocket, 23 April-2 May 1945 125
The Battle for Leer, 28-29 April 1945 126

Road Maps

The Scheldt Estuary 40
Ijzendijke 44
Woensdrecht 70

Introduction

This book and our companion volumes are designed to inspire Canadians to visit the battlefields in Europe where some of the most important chapters in our history took place. This guide focuses on some of the most significant but least-known campaigns of the Second World War in Belgium, the Netherlands and Germany.

This book is an update of the appropriate sections of our 2005 publication *The Canadian Battlefields in Northwest Europe, 1944-1945: A Visitor's Guide.* The text is by Terry Copp, the photos, maps, captions and design by Mike Bechthold. The authors wish to thank Linda Copp, Paula Fletcher, Michelle Fowler, Geoff Hayes, Mark Humphries, Andrew Iarocci, Marc Milner, David Patterson, Evert Stieber, Ralph Trost, Lee Windsor and Jim Wood for their contributions to our project.

The original guidebooks, released in 1994 and 1995, were joint publications of the Laurier Centre for Military Strategic and Disarmament Studies and the Canadian Battle of Normandy Foundation, now the Canadian Battlefields Foundation. The new series, launched in 2004, was made possible through the generosity of John and Pattie Cleghorn who offered financial support and encouragement allowing our Centre to develop an ambitious publication program. We are also grateful to Peter Kenny and the Kenny Family Foundation, the late George Gale and others who have contributed to the work of the Centre. For information about our organization visit:

www.canadianmilitaryhistory.ca

* * * * *

The Canadian battlefields in Belgium, the Netherlands and Germany are less well known than those in France, but they are an equally important part of our national history. This guide provides an introduction to the role played by First Canadian Army in the last nine months of the war in Northwest Europe.

All the Canadian battlefields described in this guide may be visited from two or three strategically located cities. We recommend Brugge (Bruges), Belgium as a base for Ieper (Ypres) and the Scheldt Estuary, and Arnhem, Netherlands for the "Market Garden" battles and the Rhineland campaign of 1945. Groningen is a good base for exploring the last phase of the war in the northern part of the Netherlands and Germany. Schipol Airport outside Amsterdam is the most obvious port of entry unless you are also visiting the battlefields of Normandy and Northern France in which case Paris - Charles de Gaulle is recommended.

When we first published these guides the internet was in its infancy. Today all travellers should use the internet to find information on hotels, restaurants and other vital information by city and region. Air tickets and car rentals are easily arranged online. If you decide to use a travel agent do your own research first.

If you would like further advice about specific places or events please contact us directly at tcopp@wlu.ca or mbechthold@wlu.ca. Our website <www.canadianmilitaryhistory.com> now includes a tab for our guidebooks that will link you to recommended sites for both historical and tourist information.

The troop transport SS *Pasteur* arrives in Halifax on 30 June 1945 to repatriate Canadian soldiers from Europe.
Canadian Forces Joint Imagery Centre ZK 1004-1

The Strategic Debate in September 1944

Generals propose: battles dispose; the battle of Normandy was no exception. Some of it had gone according to plan, but no one had envisaged a long costly stalemate followed by a situation so fluid that everything seemed possible, even a quick thrust to Berlin to end the war. The Overlord plan had called for a steady advance to the Seine and a regrouping of the Allied armies along the river before another well-prepared advance was attempted. As it was, a US division crossed the Seine on 19 August and by the 25th Paris had been liberated, and General George Patton's Third Army had crossed the upper Seine in no less than four places. The re-organization of the Allied armies would have to be done on the move.

The bitter and costly battle which the Allies had fought in Normandy created considerable tension among the military leaders. Supreme Allied Commander General Dwight D. Eisenhower's relationship with Field Marshal Bernard Montgomery, commander of 21 Army Group, had not yet deteriorated to the crisis point but most senior American officers believed that Eisenhower should quickly assume direct command of land operations and free their armies from Montgomery's control. Patton and his

A Canadian column on the move through France following the collapse of the German defences in Normandy.
Canadian Forces Joint Imagery Centre (CFJIC) ZK 928-1

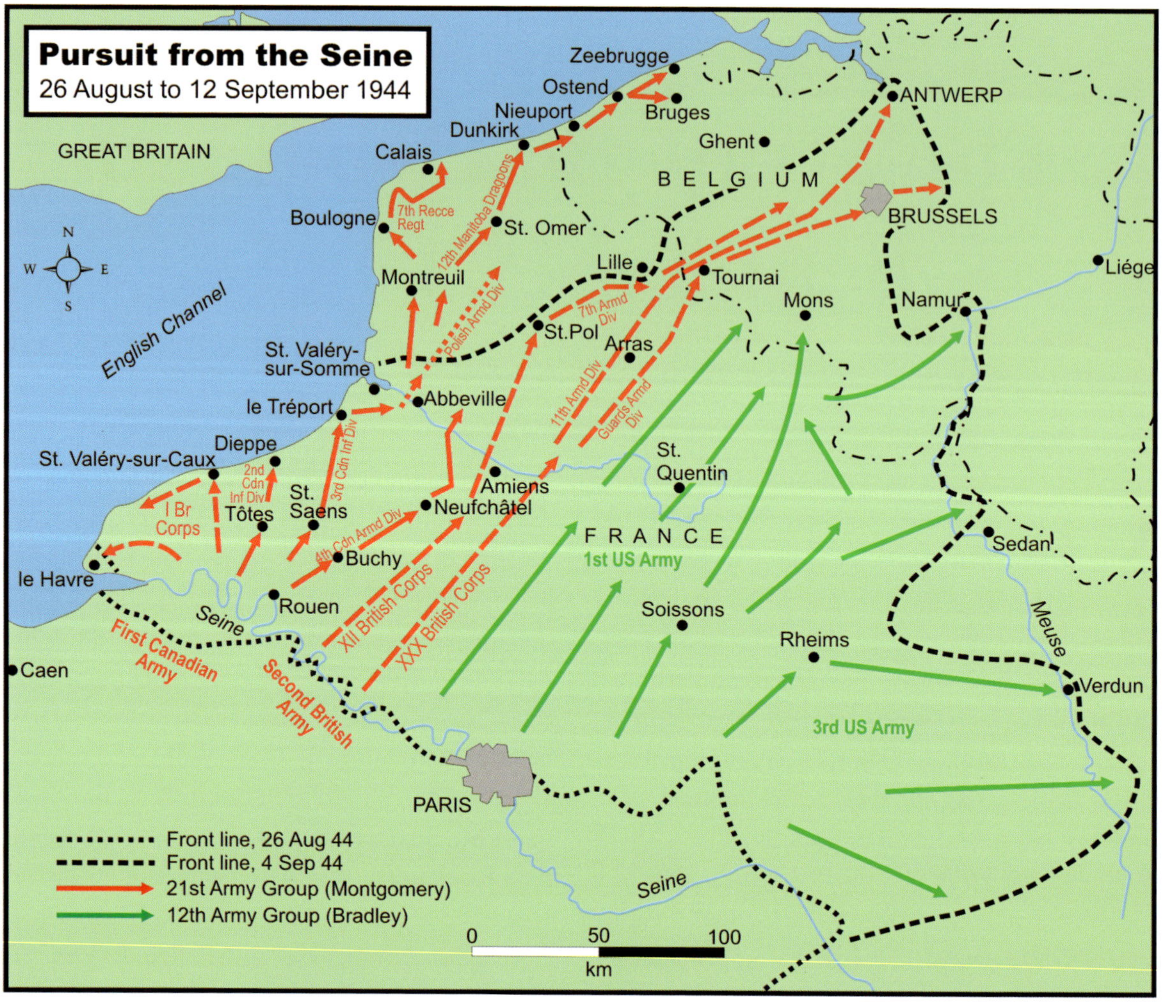

Third Army staff were particularly obsessed with "Ike's 'kowtowing' to Monty," but even General Omar Bradley, commander of 12th US Army Group, who had (on the whole) worked well with Montgomery in Normandy, was determined to end the British general's control of strategy.

It is easy to exaggerate the importance of this conflict among the generals and to see it as a cause, rather than an effect. An examination of the situation confronting the Allies in late August suggests that the strategic debate was the product of sincere and legitimate differences of opinion over a variety of strategic options, each of which had considerable merit.

As early as 17 August Montgomery had talked to General Omar Bradley about a plan which would keep the two Army Groups together advancing on a north-easterly axis with all available divisions. This was the opening move in what was to become Montgomery's obsession – the narrow front strategy of a "forty division" thrust into the heart of Germany. On 17 August the proposal had much to recommend it, although there were not 40 divisions available, logistical considerations apart.

The whole proposal should be understood in the context of the question – how best to pursue a beaten enemy in a war which nearly everyone assumed would be over by Christmas. Monty's answer was to obtain victory through a manoeuvre which would establish the air force in Belgium, secure bridgeheads over the Rhine and seize the Ruhr, the industrial district without which Germany could not survive. The plan had the added advantage of ensuring that the coastal launching sites of the V-1s would be overrun on the way to Germany and London freed from this renewal of the Blitz.

Whatever the theoretical merits of the plan, and there were strong logistical as well as purely strategical arguments against it, the real weakness was that Patton's Third US Army and a large part of First US Army had broken out of the Normandy bridgehead and were advancing out into the interior of France while Montgomery's 21st Army Group was still locked into the last stages of the Falaise battle. There was, of course, the additional problem of the future role of the Seventh US Army which was ashore in the south of France.

This should have been evident to Montgomery by 23 August when, in a further discussion with Bradley, he found the American general firmly opposed to any "single thrust" plan which the events of the past week had simply made impractical. Montgomery, convinced that only his plan could ensure victory in 1944, took his case to Eisenhower.

From the Supreme Commander's perspective, the most urgent problem facing the Allies in late August was the rapidly deteriorating supply situation. As the supply lines stretched further and further from the Normandy beaches, the problem of supplying the advancing troops with gasoline, food and ammunition was rapidly becoming unmanageable. With the French railway system still in chaos virtually all supplies had to be brought forward by truck and there were not enough trucks.

The supply situation made the decision about how to pursue the Germans difficult. Leaving logistics aside, the best bet in the last week of August was surely to reinforce success and give Third US Army priority. But a supply crisis was almost inevitable unless ports could be obtained before the fall storms could choke off supply over the Normandy beaches. The only port which had both the capacity and location to satisfy the needs of the advancing Allied armies was Antwerp. Eisenhower saw the advance along the northeast corridor to secure Antwerp as the principal offensive operation for early September. He confirmed his commitment to the northern offensive by allotting his strategic reserve, First Allied Airborne Army, to Montgomery "to expedite the accomplishment of its assigned mission." Eisenhower had not accepted Montgomery's single thrust to the Ruhr but he had placed the priority on the coastal ports and especially Antwerp, as a necessary preliminary to a broad front approach to the Rhine. Unfortunately he failed to enforce this directive.

While the Germans struggled to stop Patton's advance, Second British Army and the left wing of First US Army were charging ahead. British 30th Corps reached Amiens early on 31 August breaching the Somme "line" and moving off for Belgium. On their right two US Corps were converging on Tournai and Mons where, on 3 September, some 25,000 Germans were trapped. The British reached Brussels that same day. Opposition was negligible and as the Belgian cities were liberated, the leading armoured divisions seemed to be almost on a victory parade rather than a battlefield. On 4 September the 11th Armoured Division burst into Antwerp. There was virtually no German opposition and the well-organized Belgian resistance seized control of the vital docks. Antwerp, the largest port in Europe, was in Allied hands without a major battle and without damage to the port. Surely the German army was all but finished.

Personnel of the Belgian White Brigade in a village north of Antwerp, 17 September 1944. These partisans and their comrades played a key role in preventing the destruction of the Antwerp dockyard by the retreating Germans.
Library and Archives Canada (LAC) PA 13120 Photo by Ken Bell

The fall of Antwerp created a new situation for both the German and the Allied commands. The Germans needed to solve three separate but closely related problems if they hoped to minimize the sudden loss of the city. They needed first to improvise some defences along the river and canal systems of northern Belgium and Holland; secondly, they needed to find a way of extricating the Fifteenth Army which was pinned to the coast and cut off from all land routes to Germany since Antwerp had fallen; thirdly, they had to find ways of continuing to deny the Allies as many deep water ports as possible, particularly Antwerp.

The 15th Army had been ordered to attempt a breakout by attacking across the rear of the Second British Army as a result of the British capture of Brussels and Antwerp. It was a venture that promised little success because the pressure from the Canadians to the south would have forced the retreating Germans to fight in two directions at the same time. Moreover, the divisions of the Fifteenth Army, although strong in manpower, did not have the fire power or the mobility to attack the British while keeping the Canadians at bay. The only other way back, however, was to evacuate across the sea from Breskens to Flushing. Flushing was on the island of Walcheren, connected by a narrow causeway to South Beveland which, in turn, had only a single, totally unprotected road leading to the mainland near Woensdrecht, a mere 15 miles north of Antwerp. The idea of evacuating a whole army across this area in the face of Allied air superiority seemed ridiculous; especially since an advance by the British a few miles north from Antwerp would have forced the Germans to use a longer and more precarious sea and land route.

Nevertheless General Gustav von Zangen, the commander of the Fifteenth Army, was ordered to evacuate his army along this route and bring it as quickly as possible into line along the Albert Canal north of Antwerp. In September, the Army began to sort out its three corps and an orderly, indeed a very skilful, retreat took place. When the operation was complete on 23 September the Germans had moved 90,000 men, 600 guns, 6,200 vehicles and the same number of horses across the ferries from

Lieutenant-General Guy Simonds, commander of 2nd Canadian Corps.
CFJIC ZK 797-D

Breskens and Terneuzen through Walcheren and these troops had substantially strengthened the line north of Antwerp.

Moreover, Fifteenth Army was ordered to strengthen the garrisons of the Channel ports and to create two new 'fortresses,' Scheldt Fortress North and Scheldt Fortress South. Each fortress was each given a full division, the 64th at Breskens and the 70th on Walcheren. Well dug-in with a large supply of ammunition, protected by water obstacles, these fortress positions would prove difficult to destroy. And as long as either existed, the port of Antwerp was useless because the coastal guns commanded the estuary of the Scheldt.

The fall of Antwerp galvanized the German command into making a series of decisions which substantially changed the battle in the north. It brought no comparable changes to the Allied conception of the campaign. On 4 September Eisenhower issued a directive which began with the words "Enemy resistance on the entire front shows signs of collapse." Montgomery did not differ from Eisenhower in his appreciation of the state of the enemy, but he was convinced that there "were not enough resources for two full-blooded thrusts," and told Eisenhower that "we have now reached a stage where one really powerful and full-blooded thrust toward Berlin is likely to get there and thus end the German war." Eisenhower replied the same day, 5 September, reiterating his intention "to occupy the Saar and the Ruhr and by the time we have done this, Havre and Antwerp should be available to maintain one or both thrusts you mention. In this connection I have always given and still give priority to the Ruhr…Please let me know at once your further maintenance requirements for the advance to and occupation of the Ruhr."

Montgomery wrote back, "I submit with all respect…that a reallocation of our resources of every description would be adequate for one thrust to Berlin." Eisenhower was anxious not to see the dispute aggravated, especially since it was only a week since he had taken over the ground command. He flew to see Montgomery in Brussels on 10 September. At the end of the meeting Eisenhower agreed to an airborne operation with Arnhem as its immediate objective.

Field Marshal Bernard L. Montgomery, commander of 21st Army Group, and Lieutenant-General H.D.G. Crerar, Commander of First Canadian Army.
LAC PA 145764

First Allied Airborne Army had been created in August 1944 to develop plans for the strategic employment of the British and American airborne divisions in England. Both 82nd and 101st US Divisions had been restored to full strength after their D-Day exploits while the 1st British Airborne Division and the Polish Parachute Brigade were ready for their first operation. A third US division, 17th Airborne, was in the final stages of training and 6th British Airborne was returning to England for rest and reinforcement.

This large force of highly mobile but lightly armed soldiers were the Supreme Commander's only strategic reserve and he was under enormous pressure to employ them in large scale operations that would justify the enormous resources allocated to these elite troops. Described as "coins burning holes in SHAEF's pocket," the airborne divisions were to be used in an ambitious operation to seize a series of canal and river crossings, laying down an

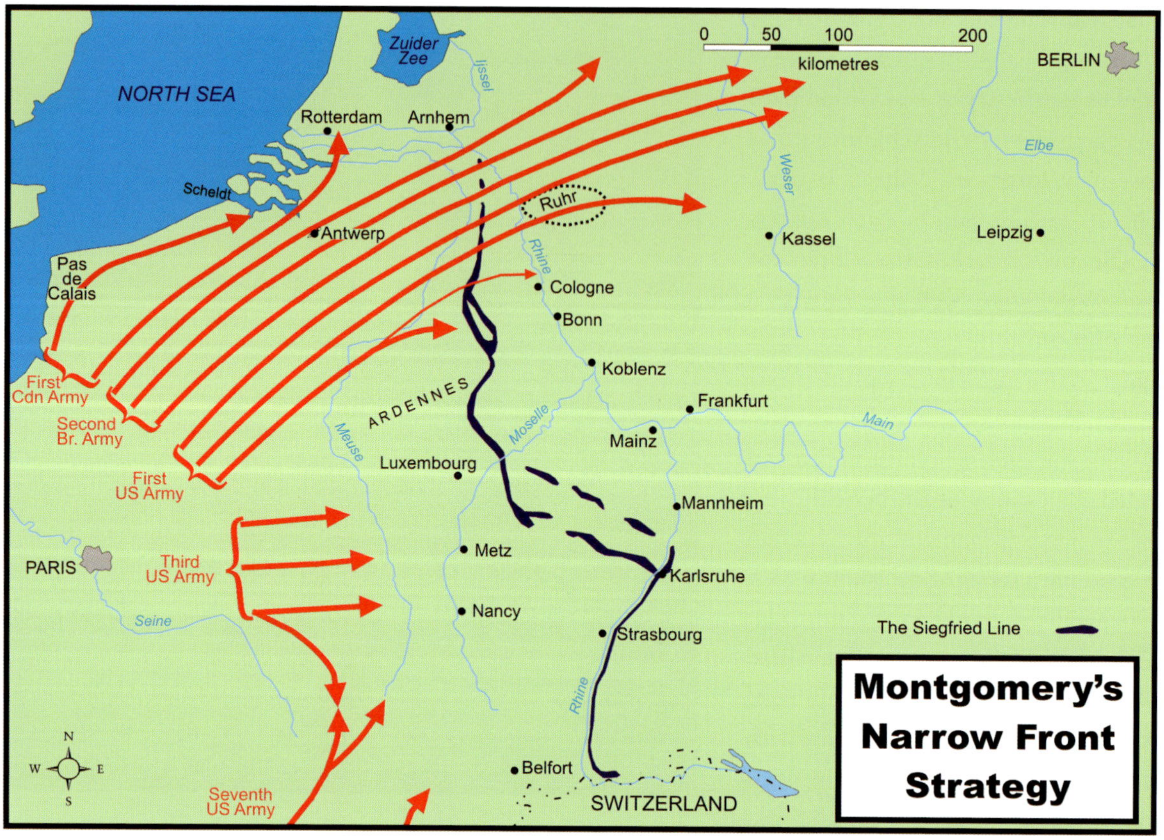
NORTH SEA
Zuider Zee
Ijssel
0 50 100 200
kilometres
BERLIN
Rotterdam
Arnhem
Elbe
Weser
Scheldt
Ruhr
Antwerp
Kassel
Leipzig
Pas de Calais
Rhine
Cologne
Bonn
Koblenz
First Cdn Army
Second Br. Army
ARDENNES
Frankfurt
Main
Meuse
Moselle
Mainz
Luxembourg
First US Army
Mannheim
Metz
PARIS
Third US Army
Karlsruhe
Nancy
Seine
Strasbourg
The Siegfried Line
Rhine
Belfort
Seventh US Army
SWITZERLAND
Montgomery's Narrow Front Strategy

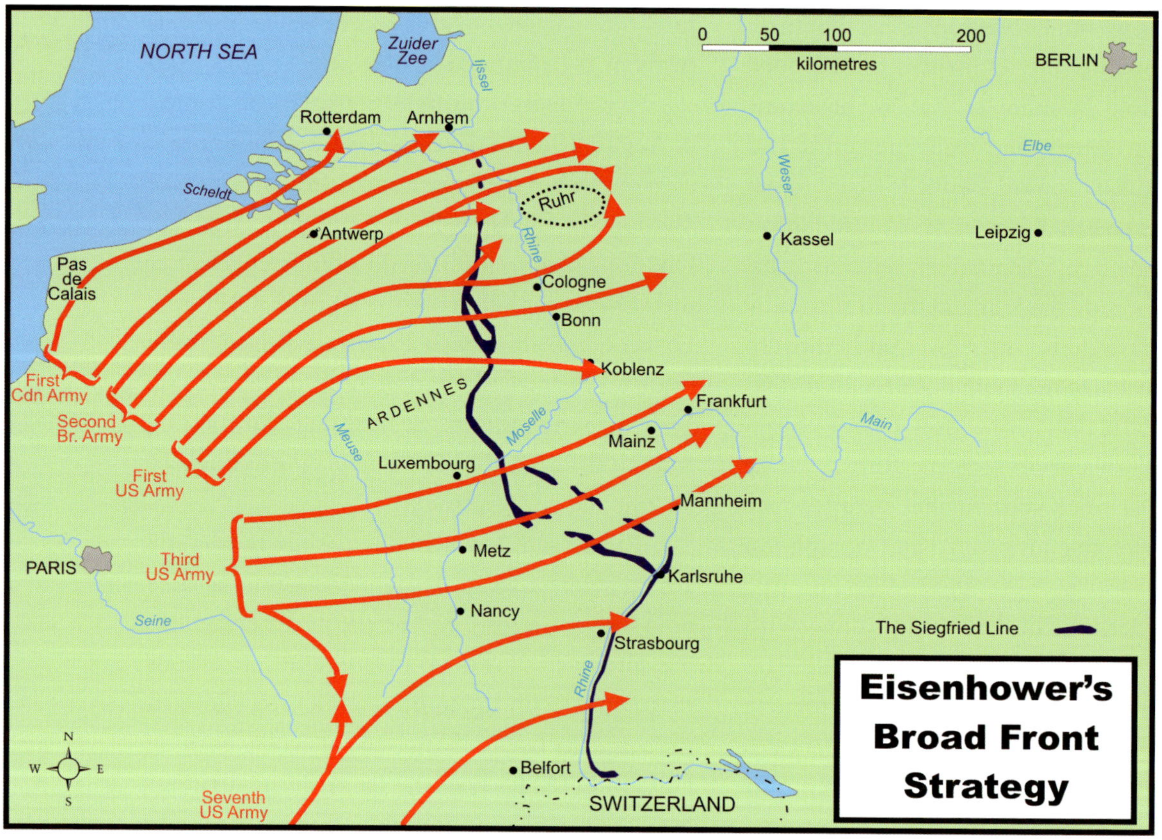
NORTH SEA
Zuider Zee
Ijssel
0 50 100 200
kilometres
BERLIN
Rotterdam
Arnhem
Elbe
Weser
Scheldt
Ruhr
Antwerp
Kassel
Leipzig
Pas de Calais
Rhine
Cologne
Bonn
Koblenz
First Cdn Army
Second Br. Army
ARDENNES
Frankfurt
Main
Meuse
Moselle
Mainz
Luxembourg
First US Army
Mannheim
Metz
PARIS
Third US Army
Karlsruhe
Nancy
Seine
Strasbourg
The Siegfried Line
Rhine
Belfort
Seventh US Army
SWITZERLAND
Eisenhower's Broad Front Strategy

airborne carpet for British Second Army's advance to the Rhine.

A smaller operation code named "Comet" had been developed in early September when a German collapse seemed certain. By 10 September with enemy resistance beginning to strengthen "Comet," a one-division airborne assault, became a three-division operation code named "Market Garden." Despite a shortage of time for planning and new intelligence about the presence of German armoured divisions in the Arnhem area, Montgomery, convinced that the war could be won in 1944, remained committed to a deeply flawed plan. Those who suggested that "Market Garden" was bound to fail unless organized German resistance had ceased to matter and those who thought that at a minimum Arnhem was a "bridge too far" were ignored. Operation "Market Garden" became the major Allied offensive of autumn 1944.

Eisenhower knew that Operation "Market Garden" would postpone the clearing of the Scheldt. He wrote to the US Chief of Staff, General George Marshall on the 14th, "I have sacrificed a lot to give Montgomery the strength he needs… It should be successful in carrying Montgomery up to and across the Rhine; thereafter it is absolutely imperative that he quickly capture the approaches to Antwerp, so that we may have use of that port." But how did Eisenhower envisage the quick capture of the approaches to Antwerp? He seems to have left the timing of this task entirely in Montgomery's hands and for the Field Marshal, Antwerp was not a priority.

Montgomery, desperate for the supplies that would make his 'single thrust' policy feasible, signalled to Crerar on 6 September asking for an estimate of the chances of an early capture of Boulogne. "I want Boulogne badly," he told Crerar. By 9 September 'Monty' was convinced that with "one good Pas de Calais port," additional transport and an increased airlift, he could make it to the Ruhr. Montgomery knew that the Fifteenth Army's withdrawal across the Scheldt had begun on 6 September and Ultra told the full story of the German orders to garrison the coastal "fortresses," but his reaction was to accept a long delay in the opening of Antwerp and to leave the escaping Fifteenth Army to the tactical air force.

A soldier from the 18th Armoured Car Regiment (12th Manitoba Dragoons) with some Belgian children. Blankenberqhe, Belgium, 11 September 1944. LAC PA 130264

Operation Market Garden

The story of Operation Market Garden, the "Bridge Too Far" is among the best known events of the Second World War. The major strategic deployment, the dropping of three airborne divisions along a 50 mile stretch of road, could only succeed if surprise was obtained and the armoured spearheads of British 30 Corps could link up with the lightly-armed airborne divisions before the Germans could organize serious counterattacks. Unfortunately for the British 1st Airborne Division, landing near Arnhem, the surprise was mutual. The dropzones were only a mile from the headquarters of Army Group B and in the midst of 2nd SS Panzer Corps' refitting area. The corps' two depleted armoured units, 9th and 10th SS Panzer Divisions, were available to respond swiftly to Field Marshal Model's orders.

Allied intelligence had provided ample warning that panzer units were in the Arnhem area, indeed Ultra had intercepted specific messages about 2nd SS Panzer Corps. There were other intelligence indications which confirmed this information but it was interpreted in the light of a broader intelligence estimate which emphasized the weakness, particularly in armour, of all the German panzer divisions. Throughout the first two weeks of September the idea that the Germans had little left with which to offer resistance became firmly entrenched in the minds of most Allied commanders.

British 1st Airborne Division was quickly isolated and placed under heavy pressure. Back along the highway the US 82nd Airborne Division was fighting a tough battle for Nijmegen and the US 101st Airborne Division was struggling to keep the highway north of Eindhoven open against repeated attacks from German units which included the 59th Division, recently evacuated across the Scheldt. British 30 Corps was not able to move rapidly north to link up with their comrades.

The German commanders reacted to the Arnhem operation with coolness and considerable skill. The 9th SS Panzer Division, with additional forces hastily collected, was ordered to prevent the British from seizing the Arnhem bridge with 10th SS was sent south towards Nijmegen. But the German command did not allow itself to be blinded by the immediate flashpoint of the front. OKW was quite certain that holding the Scheldt Estuary was of greater importance than an all-out fight against the salient and refused to weaken the line north of Antwerp even when limited attacks succeeded in cutting the corridor suggesting the possibility of isolating the US 82nd Division as well as the British troops at Arnhem.

In fact the Germans made no major strategic adjustments as a result of Market Garden. OKW remained uneasy about a possible landing in Holland and suggested extending the Westwall northwards, but the general tenor of Hitler's directive of 25 September was to assume that the front had been stabilized and the Germans could plan to eliminate the bulge in the Allied line.

The failure of Market Garden was obvious once the bridge at Arnhem could not be held and the decision was made to withdraw the 1st Airborne Division. The casualties in the week's fighting had been extraordinarily high: 7,500 of the 10,300 men who had gone into Arnhem, 3,500 from the two US airborne divisions, 3,700 in 30 Corps and 658 airmen. Approximately 2,500 men were rescued from the north side of the Rhine. Most of them were carried to safety by a small group of Canadians, members of the 23rd Field Company, Royal Canadian Engineers.

Note: We recommend that you use Arnhem as the base to explore the Canadian battlefields in the Rhineland. As such, you will find more information on Operation Market Garden, including the story of the Canadian role in rescuing the men of the 1st Airborne Division, in the chapter on the Rhineland and the Rhine Crossing.

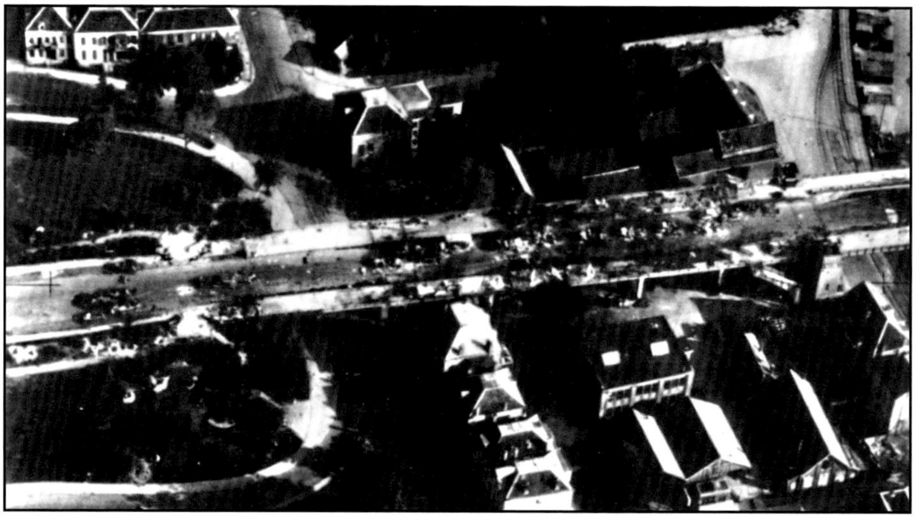

The fighting around the Arnhem bridge was vicious, as witnessed by this oblique air photo which shows the burnt-out vehicles of the German SS unit which attempted to cross the bridge held by elements of the British 1st Airborne Division.

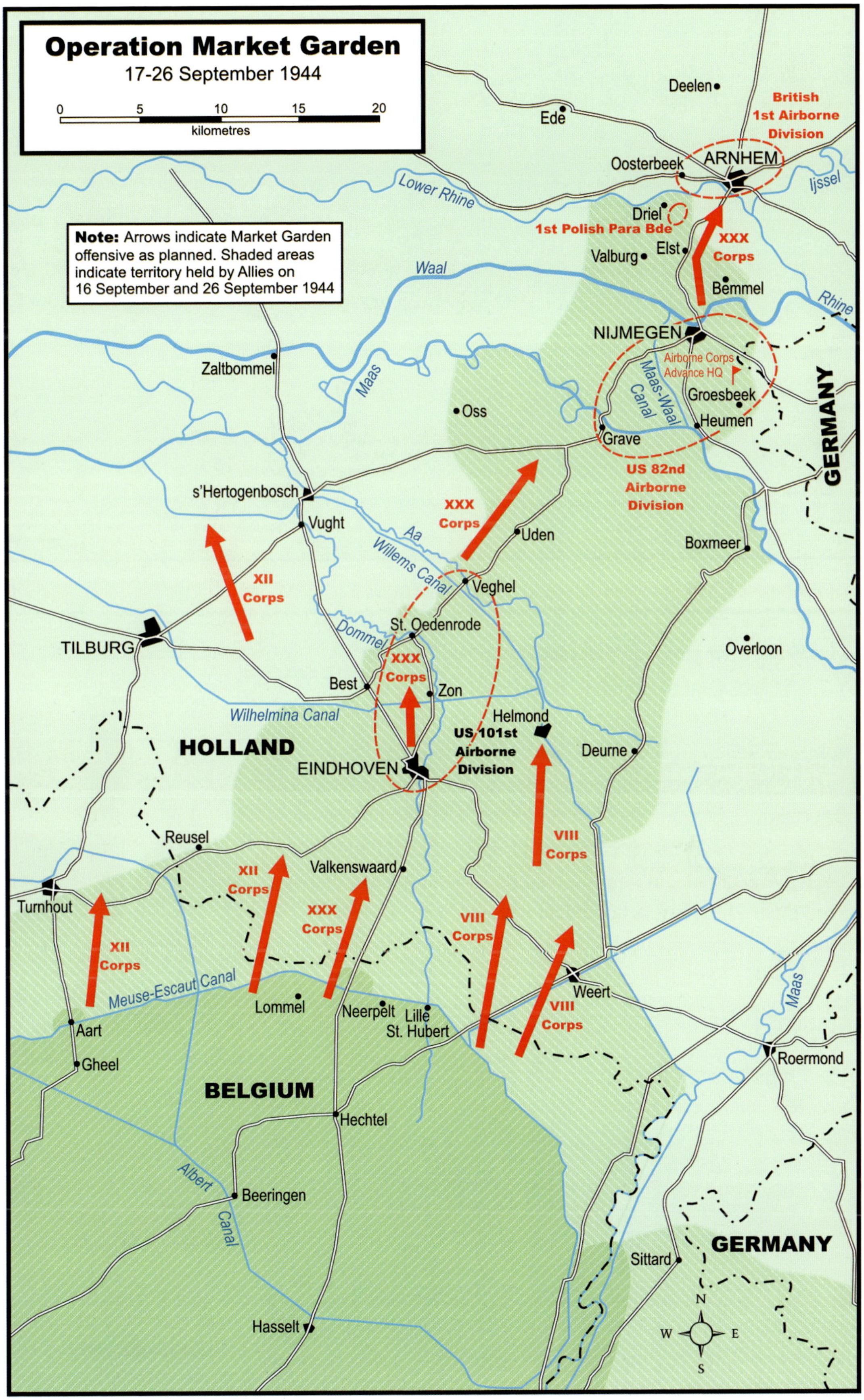
Operation Market Garden
17-26 September 1944
0 5 10 15 20
kilometres
Note: Arrows indicate Market Garden offensive as planned. Shaded areas indicate territory held by Allies on 16 September and 26 September 1944
Deelen
Ede
British 1st Airborne Division
Oosterbeek
ARNHEM
Lower Rhine
Ijssel
Driel
1st Polish Para Bde
Valburg
Elst
XXX Corps
Waal
Bemmel
Rhine
NIJMEGEN
Airborne Corps Advance HQ
Maas-Waal Canal
Groesbeek
Heumen
Grave
GERMANY
US 82nd Airborne Division
Zaltbommel
Maas
Oss
s'Hertogenbosch
Vught
Aa
Willems Canal
XXX Corps
Uden
Boxmeer
XII Corps
Veghel
St. Oedenrode
Dommel
Overloon
TILBURG
XXX Corps
Best
Zon
Wilhelmina Canal
Helmond
HOLLAND
US 101st Airborne Division
EINDHOVEN
Deurne
VIII Corps
Reusel
XII Corps
Valkenswaard
Turnhout
XXX Corps
VIII Corps
XII Corps
Meuse-Escaut Canal
Weert
Maas
Lommel
Neerpelt
Lille St. Hubert
VIII Corps
Aart
Gheel
Roermond
BELGIUM
Hechtel
Albert Canal
Beeringen
GERMANY
Sittard
Hasselt
N
W
E
S

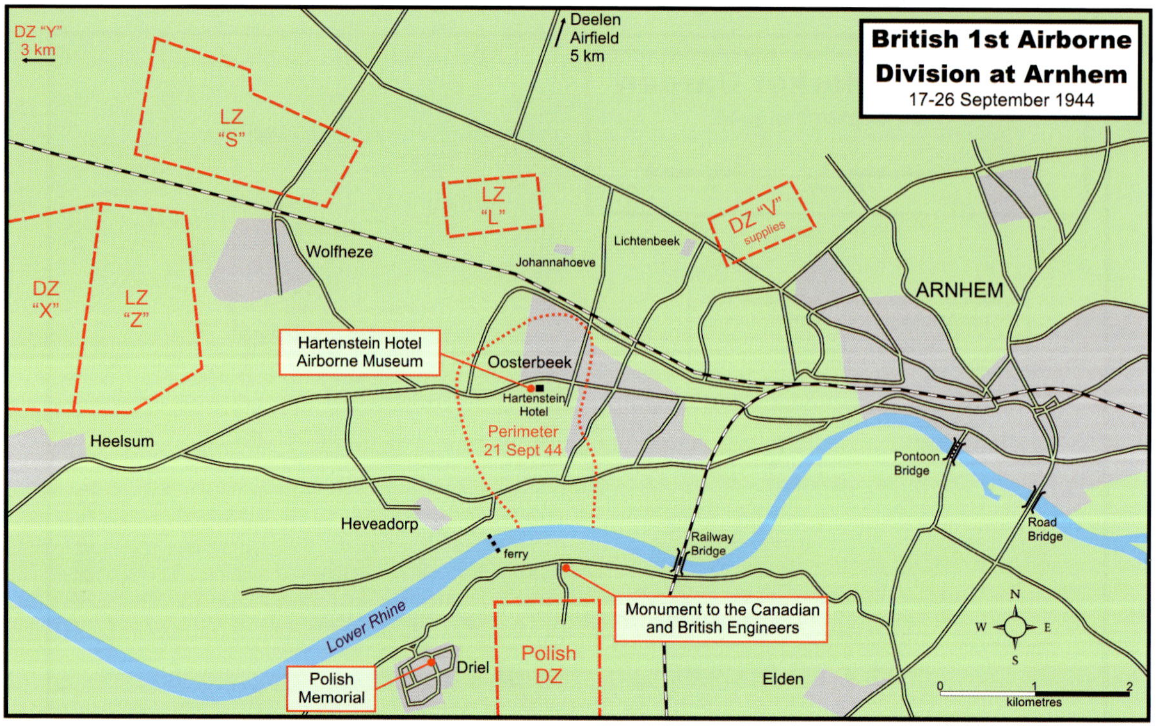

"They were just shadows and whispers in the night"

Those are the words which start the account about the evacuation of the Airborne soldiers from the Arnhem operation by men of the 20th and 23rd Field Companies Royal Canadian Engineers and the 260th & 553rd Field Companies Royal Engineers. On the night of 25 September 1944 they employed stormboats to evacuate some 2,400 to 2,500 men. In part, the report by the Major M.L. Tucker, commander of the 23rd Field Company, reads: *"The night was intensely dark, but fires started by our bombers in the afternoon and the numerous flares sent up by the enemy must have revealed a great deal of our movement to him….There was a great deal of enemy fire during the night. Machine-guns set on fixed lines swept the river and beaches on both sides….Mortar and 88-mm fire fell everywhere….A corporal operating a boat which was leaking badly decided he could make one more trip and bring off a few men before it went down. It sunk as it approached the south shore, but fortunately the water was shallow and they were able to wade ashore safely….All of the boat crews were magnificent, and only gave up their ferrying when their boats were no longer operable or else when they were exhausted and had to be ordered from the beach."*

The monument was erected in 1989 to express the gratitude of the airborne troops to their rescuers who they had never been able to thank. The memorial is on the south bank of the Rhine near Driel, directly across the river from the old church in Oosterbeek. The monument is on the south side of the road before Driel. In the village itself, there is a memorial to the Polish Airborne Brigade which was sent in to help the 1st British Airborne.

The memorial to the Canadian and British Engineers who rescued the Airborne soldiers from the Oosterbeek perimeter. The bridge at Arnhem is visible behind the memorial.

Belgium and the Breskens Pocket

Flanders

While Montgomery and Eisenhower debated strategy, the 4th Canadian (Major-General Harry Foster) and 1st Polish Armoured Divisions (Major-General Stanislaw Maczek) were committed to the liberation of Western Belgium. The British 7th Armoured Division handed over Ghent to the Poles and Major-General Maczek's men began the task of clearing the area between Ghent and Antwerp. Fourth Canadian Division was ordered to clear the Belgian coast and "pursue the enemy to the area of Eecloo."

Major-General Foster organized his division into two commands: "Moncel Force" named after Brigadier R.W. Moncel and "Stewart Force" named for the Acting CO of the 10th Infantry Brigade, Lieutenant-Colonel J.D. Stewart of the Argylls. The Corps' armoured car regiment, the 12th Manitoba Dragoons, was to provide deep reconnaissance and contact with the 1st Polish Armoured Division.

Initially, the move north went easily but Moncel Force found Bergues well defended and Foster ordered that it be left for the 2nd Division to deal with. The Manitoba Dragoons liberated Ostend without a battle, but Zeebrugge remained

The German bunker that caused so much trouble for the Regina Rifles and the Royal Montreal Regiment during their assault crossing on 6 October 1944 still stands guard on the north side of the Leopold Canal.
Photo by Linda Copp

in enemy hands. "Moncel Force" moved north into Belgium, arriving near Bruges on 8 September. Patrols from the Lake Superior Regiment reported bridges across the canals ringing Bruges were blown and the city was defended. The citizens pleaded with both German and Canadian commanders to avoid a battle for the splendid medieval city that had escaped destruction in the First World War. Foster agreed and ordered Stewart Force to seize a crossing at Moerbrugge, to the east of the city. No detailed plan was developed, nor was time taken to arrange artillery support. The Argylls crossed the canal in two boats borrowed from a nearby mooring. The lead company got across in good order but artillery and mortar fire rained down on the rest of the battalion. By dark three companies were holding a narrow perimeter under constant fire. During the early hours of the morning the Lincs crossed to join their comrades "under heavy fire from the flanks." Daylight on 9 September found both battalions virtually cut off, short of ammunition, and facing repeated counterattacks. It was not until the next morning after the engineers had bridged the canal that the first South Alberta Regiment (SAR) tanks crossed to support the final clearance of Moerbrugge. Casualties in this encounter had been very heavy and the position was consolidated only when the main body of German troops was ordered to withdraw behind the Leopold Canal leaving the remaining defenders of Moerbrugge to their fate.

A Canadian soldier talks to a Belgian Gendarme in Nieuport, Belgium, 9 September 1944.
LAC PA 131225

The battle for the Ghent Canal had been surprisingly difficult, but success there reinforced the view that the Germans were in full retreat. Foster now ordered Moncel Force, or more exactly its infantry battalion, the Algonquins, to undertake an immediate crossing of the double canal line at Moerkerke. Here the Leopold Canal and the Canal de Dérivation de la Lys run side by side, separated by an 18-metre wide dyke. Foster acted "in the expectation that a sudden surprise crossing would keep the enemy on the move." Forty assault boats, manned by men from the Lincs, were provided and the entire divisional artillery plus the mortars and medium machine guns of the New Brunswick Rangers were sited to assist the crossing. The armoured regiments were to provide indirect fire. Today the road which runs beside the canal in the village of Moerkerke carries the name "Algonquinstraat." In 1944 this quiet country lane was the startline for a battle which was to reveal just how committed the enemy was to the defence of the Breskens Pocket.

Shortly before midnight on the 13th all four companies of the Algonquins were ferried across the two canals under heavy harassing fire. The engineers began construction of a bridge, but small arms fire stopped the work. At first light the situation was growing desperate. Enemy artillery and mortars prevented bridging, and the shellfire, which appeared to be directed by an enemy agent, struck battalion headquarters and the Regimental Aid Post in Moerkerke. The shelling was so intense that it was impossible to get supplies of ammunition across the canal to the rifle companies which were reporting shortages. There were no additional infantry units available to reinforce or extend the bridgehead and no air support.

Opposite: This air photo details the action fought by the Algonquins in their assault crossing of the Leopold Canal, 13-14 September 1944
LCMSDS Air Photo Collection 200/4169

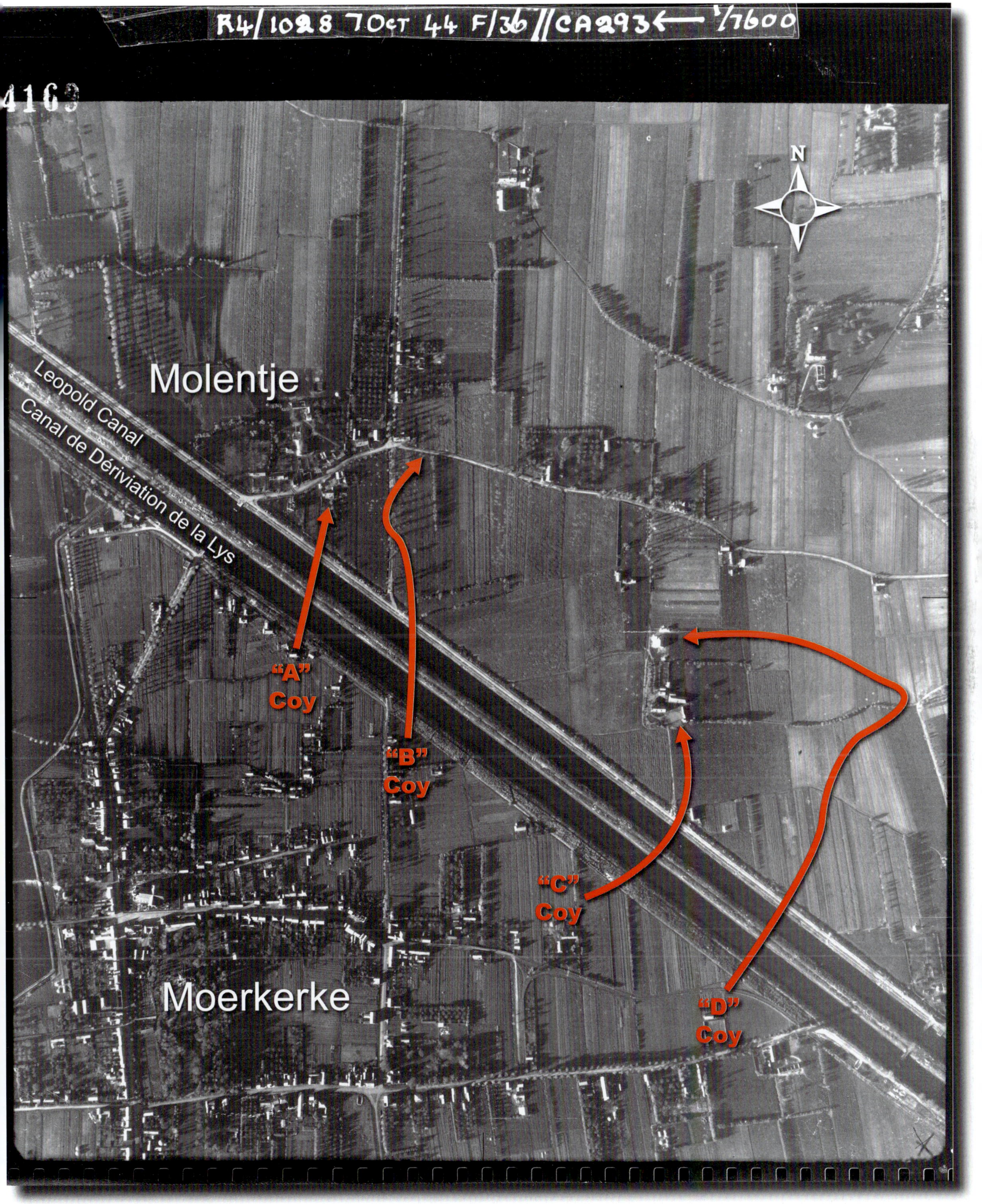
R4/1028 7 OCT 44 F/36 //CA293 ← 1/7600
4169
N
Molentje
Leopold Canal
Canal de Dériviation de la Lys
"A" Coy
"B" Coy
"C" Coy
"D" Coy
Moerkerke

Right: Private E.A. Boisvenue of the South Saskatchewan Regiment rests in Nieuport, Belgium, 9 September 1944.
LAC PA 131419

Far right: Private W.J. Forrester, RCASC (attached to the Algonquin Regiment) with members of the Belgian White Brigade, Bruges, Belgium, 13 September 1944.
LAC PA 130265

Lieutenant-Colonel R.A. Bradburn, commanding officer of the Algonquins, requested an airdrop of supplies but with Operation Market-Garden days away no aircraft were available.

With the aid of an enormous barrage and smoke screen, the Algonquins withdrew, fighting their way through pockets of enemy troops who had infiltrated as far as the island between the two canals. With most of the boats destroyed by shellfire many of the men had to swim back to the south bank, abandoning their equipment. Of the 240 men who had crossed into the bridgehead 28 were dead, 40 wounded and 66 prisoners of war.

After the disastrous attempt to rush the Leopold Canal with a single infantry battalion, the corps commander, Guy Simonds, finally accepted the intelligence derived from Ultra on Hitler's orders to hold the Scheldt fortresses. He decided that the 4th Division should confine its activities to maintaining contact and exerting pressure on the enemy. The Germans were to be left to complete their evacuation across the Scheldt, subject only to whatever harassment the Second Tactical Air Force could provide. Fourth Division therefore turned east to mop up the area between the Breskens Pocket and the Terneuzen Canal.

Maldegem and Adegem were liberated without a fight, but when the Lincs reached Eecloo excited civilians informed the battalion commander that the Germans had not yet completed evacuation of the town. Lieutenant-Colonel W.T. Cromb, commanding officer of the Lincoln and Welland Regiment, decided to obey the order not to dissipate resources by giving the Germans ample time to leave. Two days later the Lincs and a squadron of the British Columbia Regiment (BCR) advanced around the southern end of Savojaards Plaat towards Philippine. The Argylls, working with the South Alberta Regiment, also moved east in the face of flooding and roadblocks, but found scant sign of the enemy. The Algonquins and Canadian Grenadier Guards (CGG) did find resistance in Assende and were required to organize a set-piece attack with artillery support to capture the town. The Argylls crossed the Dutch border and liberated the first Dutch town freed by the Canadians, Sas-van-Gent, on 20 September. Philippine fell the same day. By nightfall on the 21st the area from Savojaards Plaat to the Terneuzen Canal was reported clear of the enemy except for a narrow neck of land encompassing the Isabella Polder. This was the only land bridge into the Breskens Pocket and the Germans were determined to defend it vigorously.

After 21 September, 4th Division took up a position along the Leopold as far west as Strooiburg while the Manitoba Dragoons, with 8th Canadian Light Anti-Aircraft Regiment under command, patrolled the area to the sea. Tenth Brigade had been told that "in view of heavy enemy opposition, their task would now be to contain the enemy and harass him with fire and by active patrolling but NO major effort should be made to dislodge him." Brigadier J.C. Jefferson, commanding officer of 10th Brigade, interpreted this direction somewhat loosely on 22 September when he ordered the Algonquin Regiment to attempt to break through the Isabella position. A two-day battle followed which inflicted heavy losses on a regiment which had just been rebuilt from reinforcement personnel.

While 4th Division masked the Leopold, the withdrawal of Fifteenth Army across the Scheldt continued. General von Zangen's account of this crossing comments on the harassing effects of Allied tactical air power, but states that the evacuation was carried out without major losses. The failure of Allied tactical air power to seriously damage the Fifteenth Army was a product of the same problem of conflicting priorities which plagued all operations in September. Second Tactical Air Force's 84 Group, which worked with First Canadian Army, was required to support operations along the Channel coast and to assist 83 Group. The Scheldt crossings were not given the priority they deserved.

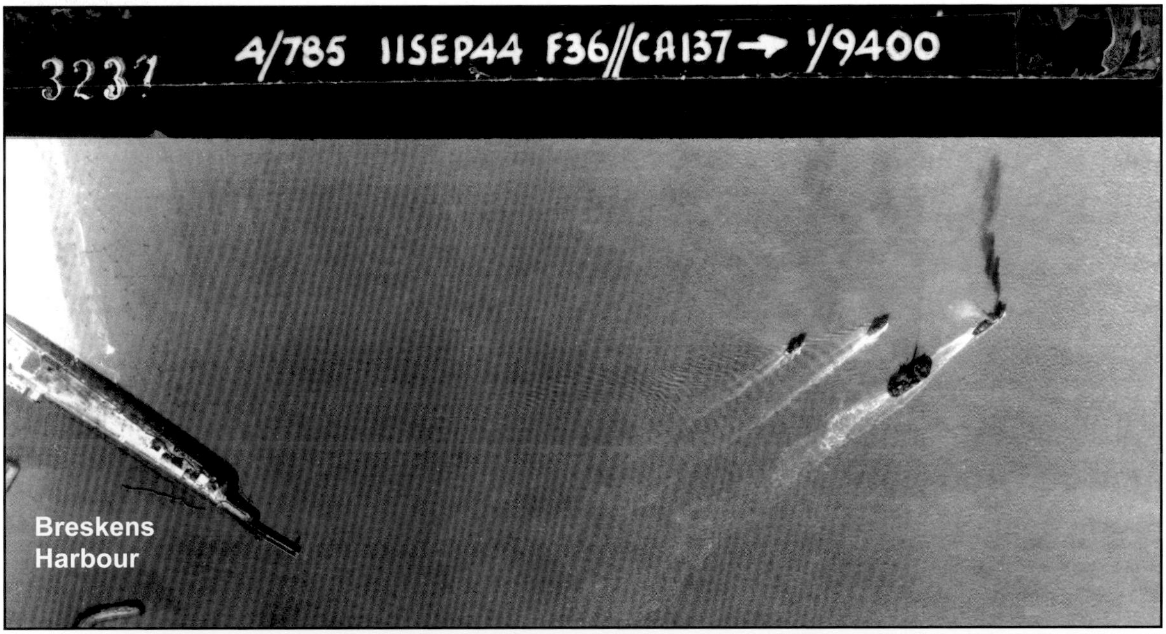

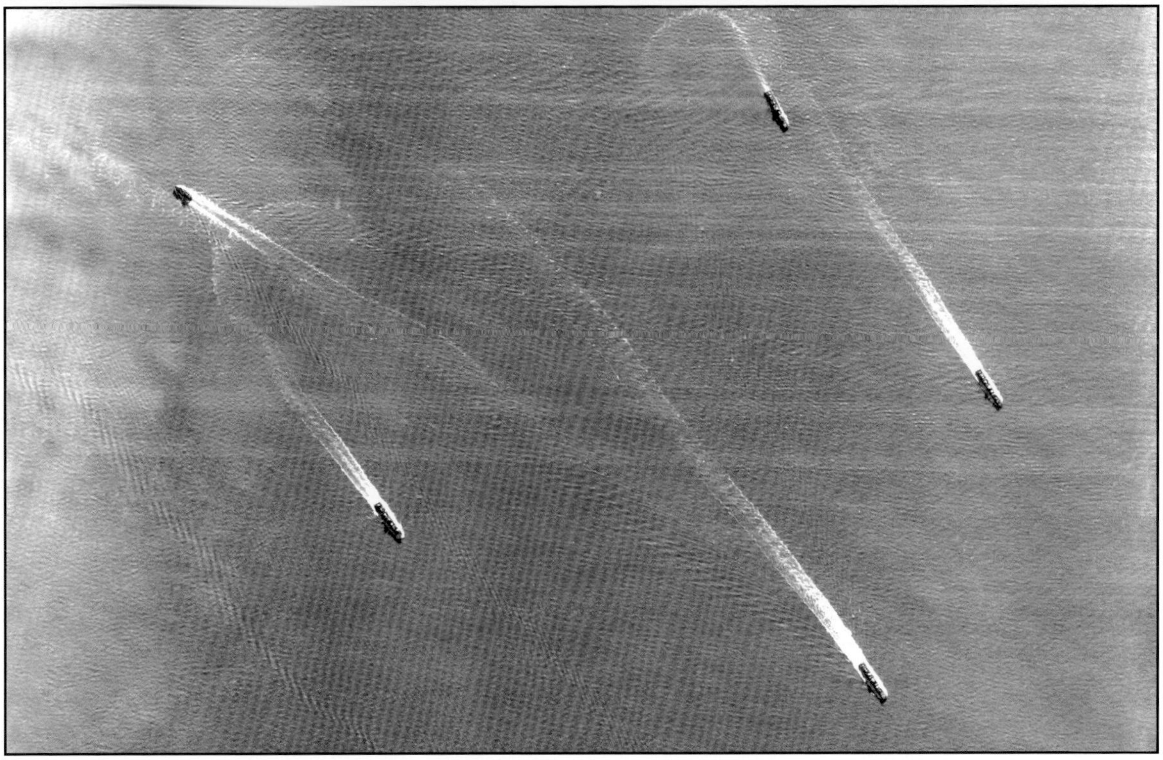

These two air photos, taken on 11 September 1944, clearly show the evacuation of the German 15th Army from the Breskens Pocket. In the upper photo, a large ship, a medium ship and two small escorts have just cleared the harbour at Breskens (visible at left). The lower photo was also taken just off Breskens harbour and shows four large vessels heading towards Vlissingen (Flushing) and one smaller vessel returning to Breskens. The Allied Air Forces, tasked with other priorities during this period, missed a golden opportunity to stem the German retreat.
LCMSDS Air Photos 159/3237 & 4239

Operation "Switchback"
The Breskens Pocket

Field Marshal Montgomery had assigned the task of clearing the Scheldt to First Canadian Army on 13 September. Between 13 September and the end of the month the planning staff at Canadian Army Headquarters and Lieutenant-General Guy Simonds (who did his own planning) discussed a variety of options on the understanding that the Scheldt was a priority operation. It gradually became apparent that, with the notable exception of Admiral Bertram Ramsey, no senior Allied commander really believed that the opening of the port of Antwerp had sufficient priority to interfere with the execution of other plans.

In mid-September Crerar had been advised that he could call upon the airborne army to support his attack on Beveland and Walcheren. The 17th US Airborne Division was said to be available immediately, with 6th British Airborne ready for action by early October. Plans were drawn up for the use of paratroops in seizing a small port on Beveland, for capturing the crossings of the Beveland Canal and for securing the Walcheren causeway. General Lewis Brereton, the commander of First Airborne Army, "with the backing of Air Chief Marshal Leigh-Mallory," convinced Eisenhower that airborne operations of this kind were "unsound." Despite strenuous attempts to reverse this decision it was not possible to overcome Brereton's opposition to the "tactical" use of his "strategic" force.

RAF Bomber Command was initially cooperative, readily agreeing to try and breach the dykes which kept Walcheren Island above the sea. The proposal to "sink" Walcheren was put forward by Simonds who argued that if the island could be flooded, the enemy's ability to defend it would be severely hampered. Bomber Command agreed to make the attempt and on 2 October warning leaflets were dropped over the island. The next day 259 Lancasters and Mosquitoes aimed more than a thousand tons of bombs at the Westkappelle dyke which was soon broken. On 7 and 11 October the RAF returned to open gaps in the dykes

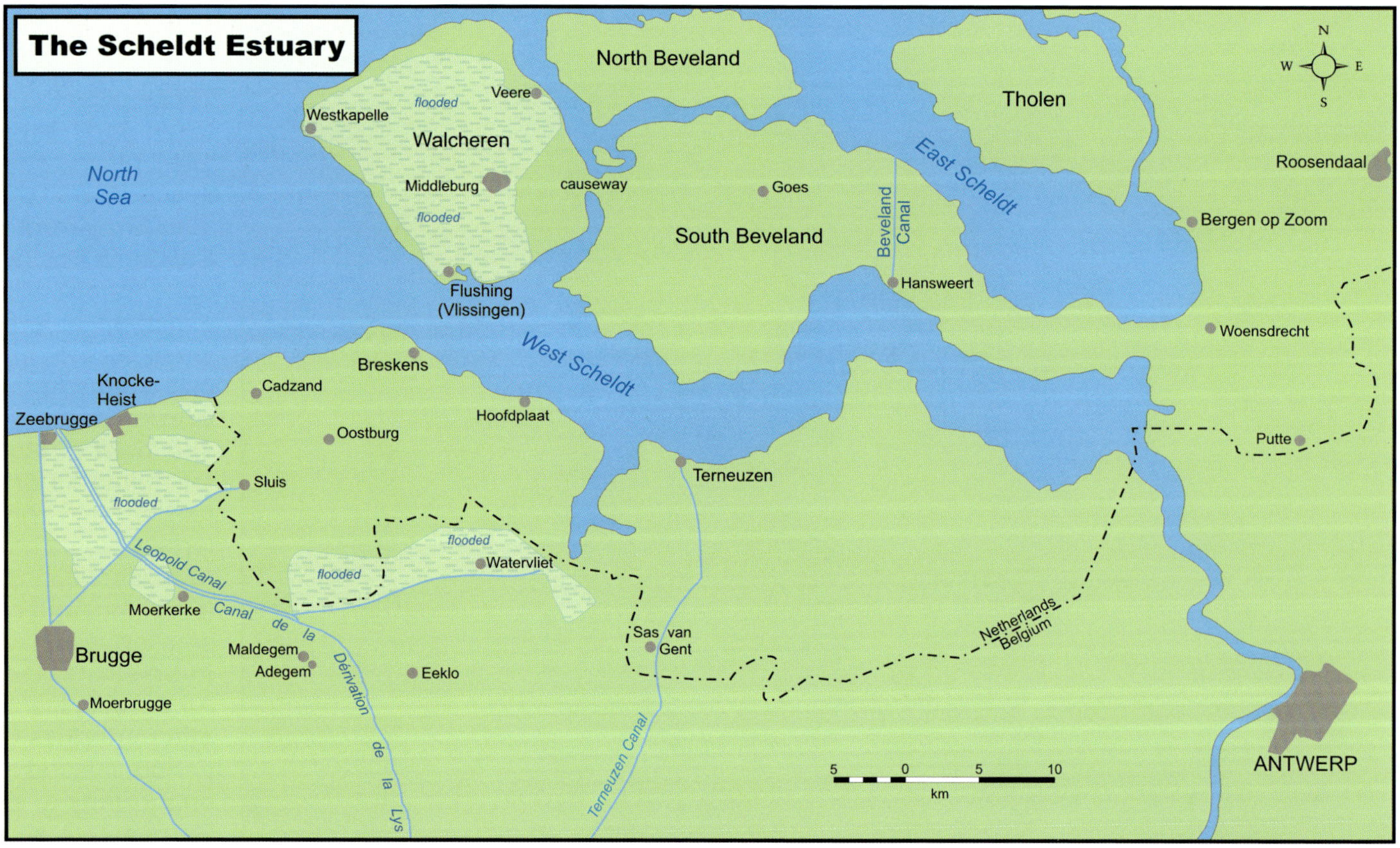

near Flushing and on the north coast at Veere. Walcheren was "sinking" beneath the waters of the North Sea.

With airborne troops unavailable, First Canadian Army would have to clear the Scheldt with its own resources. Unfortunately, the failure of Operation "Market Garden" had left Montgomery with the task of defending a long, narrow salient against repeated counterattacks. Montgomery, still determined to get to the Ruhr and quite unwilling to abandon any of the ground so dearly bought, drew upon the resources of First Canadian Army to protect and expand the left flank of the salient while Second British Army tried unsuccessfully to fight its way east. On 27 September Montgomery ordered 49th British Division, reinforced by the Sherbrooke Fusiliers of 2nd Canadian Armoured Brigade and 1st Polish Armoured Division, to advance north-eastwards toward Tilburg. Ten days later the remaining British division in First Canadian Army, 51st Highland, was brought forward to support this thrust. During the first two weeks of October these units were engaged in support of Montgomery's main effort, not operations to clear the approaches to Antwerp.

The commitment of half the resources of First Canadian Army to Second British Army also had an important effect on the tactical air power available to support operations to clear the Scheldt. An analysis of the missions undertaken by 84 Group reveals that before 16 October at least half the sorties were directed to the eastern flank. It should be noted that the weather had an even greater effect upon the availability of tactical air support in October. During the first half of the month there were just eight days in which the skies were clear and more than 400 sorties (the record was 804 on 12 October) could be flown. From 15 October to the end of the Scheldt battle, the weather all across the front made flying conditions "impossible" on six days and heavily restricted on most others.

On 26 September, General Harry Crerar, plagued by persistent dysentery and anaemia, nominated Lieutenant-General Simonds as temporary commander of the Army while he

Lieutenant-General Guy Simonds (standing beside jeep) confers with Field Marshal B.L. Montgomery (seated).
LAC PA 129125

entered hospital in England. Simonds, at the peak of his professional career, seems to have regarded the limitations on the resources available as a challenge to his ingenuity rather than a cause for concern. He told his officers: "there is no task which can be dismissed as impossible and since this particular one has been assigned to us, it is necessary to evolve methods which seem to offer the best prospects of success."

Simonds believed that Walcheren Island would be the really difficult battle. The tasks of clearing the Breskens Pocket and occupying South Beveland were regarded as preliminary operations which could be handled quickly by his two infantry divisions. The fact that 2nd Division would fight north from Antwerp with only one armoured regiment, the Fort Garry Horse, and 3rd Division would be without tank support seems to have been accepted as inevitable at Army and Corps headquarters. When the First Hussars were brought forward from Calais in October they too were assigned to 1st British Corps.

The supply situation, which had required 4th Armoured Division to assume a static role in mid-September, was to control deployment of this formation until mid-October. First Canadian Army loyally accepted the priority accorded Second British Army and planned the clearance of the Scheldt on the assumption that 4th Division could only be used to hold the eastern end of the Breskens pocket and undertake feint attacks in support of 3rd Division. This meant that there was no significant role for the fuel-starved armoured brigade. Infantry battalions would be required to patrol and the artillery would be used to support 3rd Division, but the war diaries leave no doubt that most of 4th Division was forced to wait and watch until the Scheldt was accorded greater priority.

Field Marshal Montgomery wrote in his *Memoirs*, "I must admit a bad mistake on my part; I underestimated the difficulties of opening up the approaches to Antwerp so that we could get free use of that port. I reckoned that the Canadian Army could do it while we were going for the

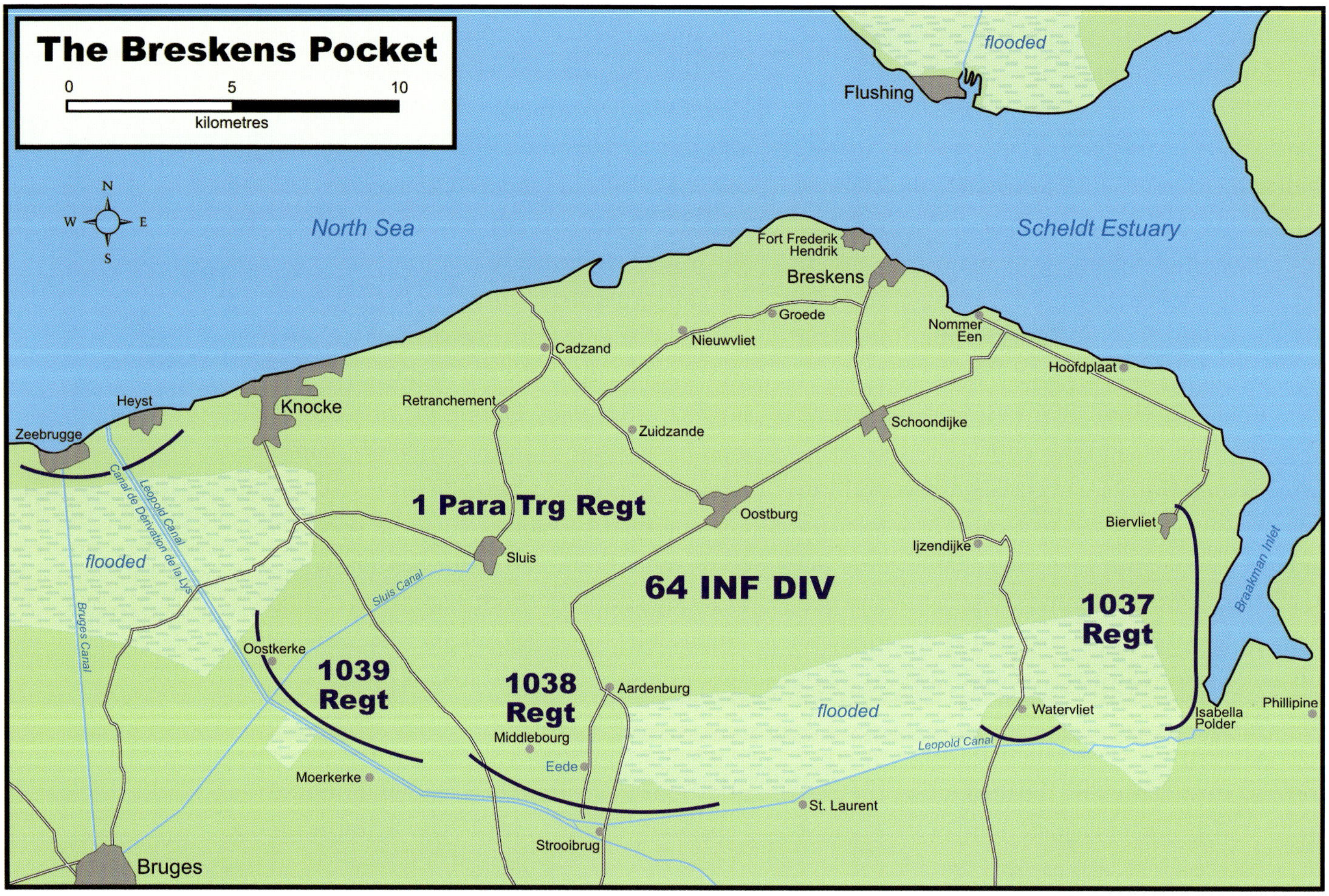

Ruhr. I was wrong." Montgomery was wrong, as we shall see, but it is important to recognize that First Canadian Army, or at least Guy Simonds, did not challenge Montgomery's belief that both jobs could be done with the available resources.

* * * * *

General Gustav von Zangen selected 64th Infantry Division to defend "Fortress South Scheldt" because, in his words "it was the only division still maintaining its full fighting power, both as to its strength and equipment and above all, it was commanded in a very efficient way."

The division had been formed in the summer of 1944 with its cadres made up of veteran officers and NCOs on leave from the eastern front. The ranks of the 64th had been filled with whoever was available, including a number of overage men, but its commander, Major-General Knut Eberding, was a vigorous 45-year old professional infantryman with considerable experience of defensive warfare in Russia. Von Zangen further noted, "the fighting quality of this Division was increased considerably by the fact that formations of the other divisions, which were taken across the Scheldt, left behind war material of all kinds, including artillery guns, antitank guns, ammunition and also food supplies." Fifteenth Army reported that it had left the Breskens area to be defended by 300 officers and 10,700 men.

Eberding and his men were also fortunate in having nearly three weeks to prepare the defences of the Leopold Canal without significant interference from the Allied air forces or the Canadian army. The division's three grenadier regiments were placed along the north bank of the Leopold. The one land bridge onto the "island," the area of the Isabella Polder, was especially heavily manned.

Eberding later claimed to have considered the possibility of an amphibious assault on his left flank but assumed it could only be on a small scale across the Braakman Inlet. This area was assigned to a force of some 300 men with headquarters at Biervliet. The north coast was left with a scattering of guard posts. The divisional reserve was concentrated in the centre near Sluis.

Major-General Dan Spry, GOC 3rd Canadian Infantry Division (left) with the King during an investiture ceremony.
CFJIC ZK 901-1

The terrain of the pocket, "a maze of ditches, canalized rivers and commercial canals, often above the level of the surrounding countryside" made military manoeuvre almost impossible except on the narrow roads built on top of the dykes. Each of these roadways was carefully registered for both artillery and mortar fire.

The Canadian plan for clearing the Breskens Pocket, codenamed "Switchback," was a complex and original response to a difficult problem. First Canadian Army had obtained the use of a large number of "landing vehicles tracked" (LVTs) for use in the assault against Walcheren. The main vehicle, called a "Buffalo," could carry 30 men in full fighting order or alternately a load such as a Jeep, 6-pounder anti-tank gun or universal carrier. Buffaloes could enter and leave the water on any reasonable slope and could churn through all but the worst mud flats.

Simonds proposed to use the LVTs to mount an amphibious operation in the rear of the Breskens Pocket. This task was assigned to John Rockingham's "Highland" Brigade while

Right: A Buffalo LVT (Landing Vehicle Tracked) climbs the bank of the Escaut River, Belgium, 26 September 1944.
LAC PA 131236

Left: A demonstration of a Wasp flamethrower, September 1944.
CFJIC ZK 873-1

Right: A demonstration of the use of flame-throwers across a canal, Balgerhock, Belgium, 4 October 1944.
LAC PA 131240

Jock Spragge's "Western" Brigade was selected to conduct a direct attack across the Leopold Canal to focus German attention away from the assault landings. D-Day was set for 6 October. This left only four days for detailed planning, the movement of troops to concentration areas and unit briefings. Fortunately, General Hobart's invaluable 79th Armoured Division had trained five squadrons of the 5th Assault Regiment, Royal Engineers to operate the miniature armada of LVTs so that preparations could begin while 3rd Division completed the capture of Calais. Seventh Brigade had just four days to recover from the Calais operation but towards dawn on the 6th, the infantry companies of the Regina Rifles and Canadian Scottish were in position.

If 7th Brigade was ready, 9th Brigade was not. The Highland Brigade had completed the capture of Cap Gris Nez on 29 September but were not able to begin training with the Buffaloes until the 5th. It soon became clear that the operation could not be mounted in time. A decision was made to commit 7th Brigade "at first light 6 Oct." and launch 9th Brigade on the night of 7/8 October.

Staff at 3rd Division headquarters prepared a plan that would use Wasp flamethrowers in support of the 7th Brigade attack. Experiments demonstrated that when the reverse slope of the dike was used to angle the Wasp, the flame could reach the other side of the canal. Major-General Dan Spry, commander of 3rd Canadian Infantry Division, decided to use this method instead of an artillery barrage in the hope of achieving both suppression and tactical surprise. He also approved the use of a sound effects troop that was to simulate the noise of bridge building and troop movement at a potential crossing point well to the east of the real objective. Those who witnessed the trials of

Below: A scout patrol from the Canadian Scottish Regiment going out on a patrol towards the Leopold Canal, 7 October 1944.
LAC PA 142100

Below left: A scout car delivers a message to the Canadian Scottish Regiment while on patrol near the Leopold Canal, 7 October 1944.
LAC PA 142099

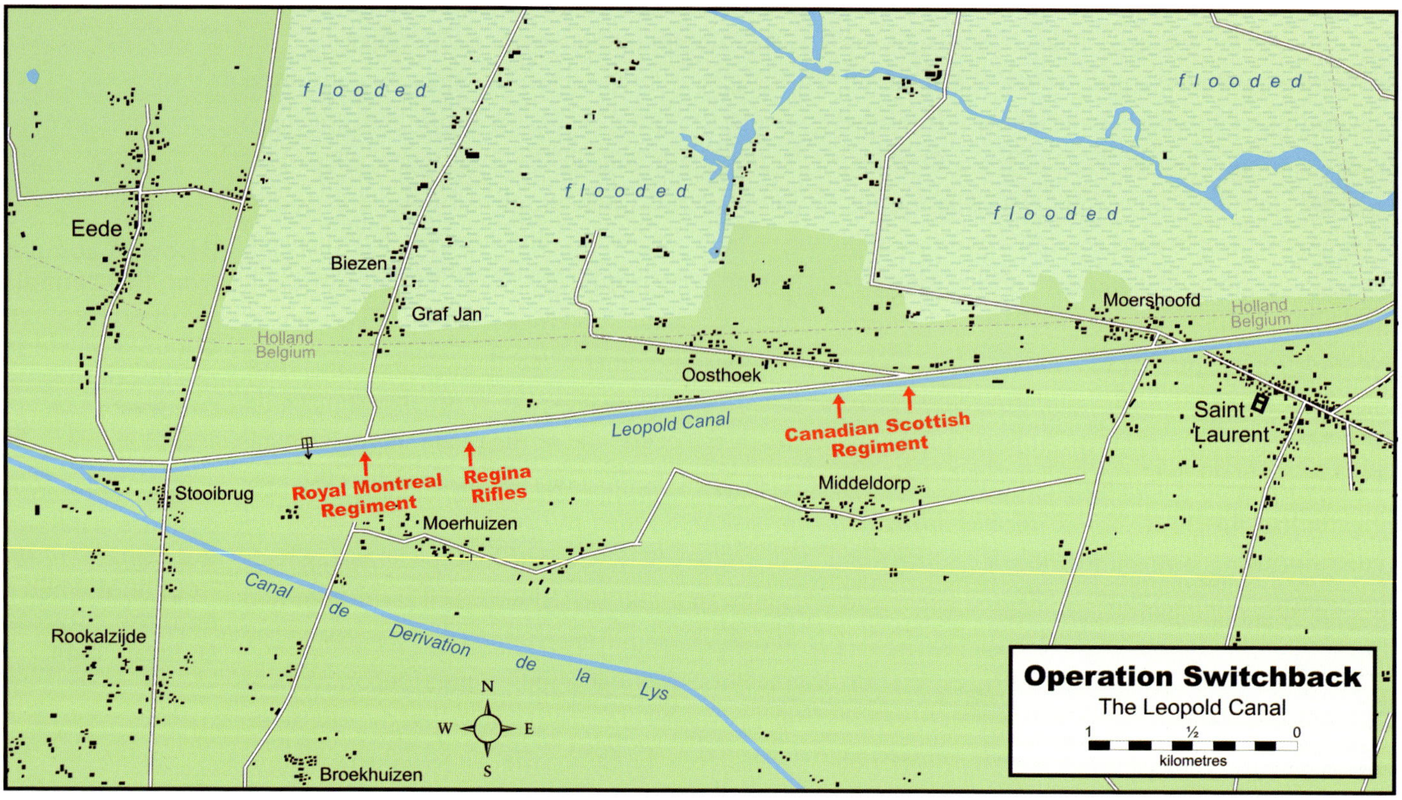

the flamethrowers were impressed and there was some hope that the shock effect would stun the enemy during the early stages of the attack.

Lieutenant-Colonel Foster Matheson's Regina Rifles drew the heavily-defended sector near the Breskens road. To make the crossing, Matheson selected his own Able Company and a company of the Royal Montreal Regiment (RMR) that had joined the battalion in September. The Royal Montreal Regiment, serving as Headquarters Defence Company at First Canadian Army, had lobbied hard for a chance to serve with a front-line battalion. Matheson had watched them closely during the fighting at Calais and was impressed with their spirit and determination. On the morning of 6 October 1944, they would need all of that determination and more.

The North Shore (New Brunswick) Regiment provided companies to man the boats and at 0525 hours the silence and darkness was broken by the roar of the flamethrowers that turned night into day. For a full five minutes the north bank was scorched and fires were still burning by the time the boats hit the water. The fires, and German flares, lit up the sky. This made it easier for enemy machine-gunners to pick out targets. One platoon of the Royal Montreal Regiment was destroyed when a "cone of fire" struck the boats. The other platoon crossed unscathed, scrambled up the bank and began to work its way westward towards the road. The commanding officer, Captain Robert Schwob, and a handful of men, including the artillery forward observation officer, clung to the north bank of the canal. They fought off a heavy counterattack and tried desperately to identify targets for the gunners.

Able Company of the Regina Rifles, attacking to the right of the RMRs, had run into concentrated fire that made crossing the canal impossible. Matheson ordered Dog Company to take over and deal with the main pillbox. Bombs from a Projector Infantry Anti-Tank (PIAT) forced the enemy to cease-fire and the company crossed and secured the area. Only 13 RMR soldiers were left and they were merged with the Regina Company whose own strength was now about 20 men.

The assault had gone much better for the Canadian Scottish Regiment. The enemy defences in the narrow end of a triangle that led nowhere were much less formidable and the crossing was

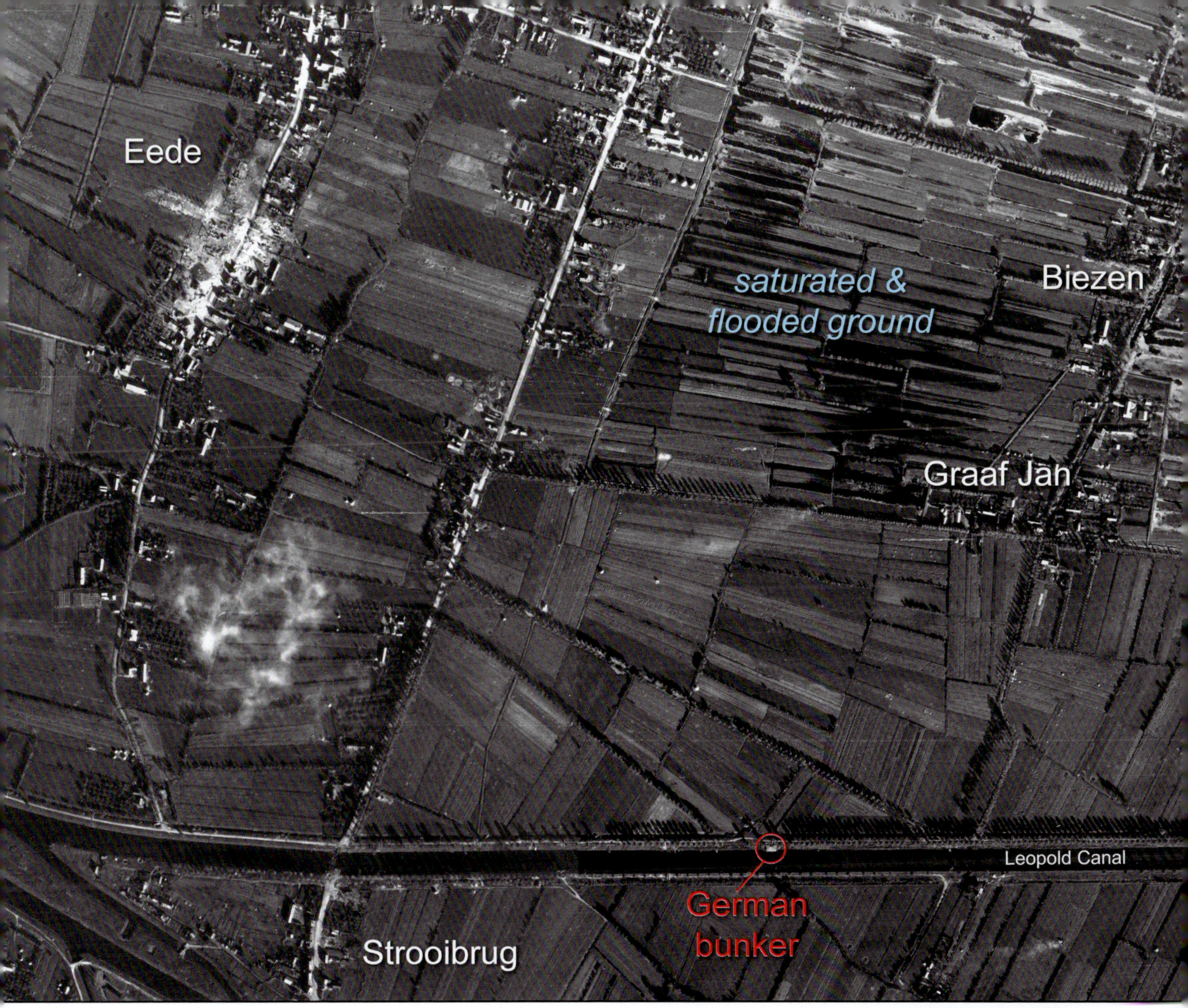

made without initial opposition. The assault companies attacked the village of Moershoofd, while the engineers built a footbridge. Soon the Canadian Scottish reserve companies were across, but attempts to move west towards Oosthoek and the Breskens road were stopped by heavy fire. The Royal Winnipeg Rifles then crossed the canal and tried to link up with the Reginas, but the volume of enemy fire made movement almost impossible. The one positive feature of this dreadful ordeal was that the enemy behaved in accordance with its doctrine and continued to counterattack with local and divisional reserves. Canadian artillery inflicted heavy casualties on the enemy who remained unaware of the threat to their rear.

The war diary of the Canadian Scottish Regiment offers a striking picture of life on the north bank of the Leopold:

> Water and soil make mud. Mud sticks to everything. Boots weigh pounds more. Rifles and Brens operate sluggishly. Ammunition becomes wet. Slit trenches allow one to get below the ground, but also contain several inches of thick water. Matches and cigarettes are unusable. So almost everyone looks for a house. A good house is one which only has a few holes in the walls and not more than half the roof dismantled. These are hard to find after our arty [artillery] has lifted its range

This air photo was taken on 6 October 1944, the first day of the 7th Brigade attack across the Leopold Canal. It shows the sector assaulted by the Royal Montreal Regiment and the Regina Rifles. The effects of Canadian defensive artillery fire are clearly visible, especially in Eede, as is the flooded ground north of the canal.
LCMSDS Air Photos 196/3047 & 3049

Right: A modern air photo of the Leopold Canal looking eastwards.

Below: A close-up of the German bunker that caused so many problems for the Canadians.
Photos by Evert Stieber

and after the enemy arty has found its range. So the soldier shakes his head, cleans his rifle, swears a good deal and dreams of what he'll do when he gets leave...."

The war diary of the Royal Winnipeg Rifles describes that unit's valiant struggle to reach the Reginas: "Heavy casualties were suffered by both sides and the ground was littered with both German and Royal Winnipeg dead....Prolonged exposure to wet and cold still had to be endured in flooded slit trenches or smashed buildings as usually bold enemy snipers and machine-gunners...succeeded in infiltrating between companies....Few of those lived to tell their story as the Royal Winnipeg Rifles were no less aggressive. Ammunition, cold rations and casualties had to be carried for more than a mile."

The men of 7th Brigade could do little more than endure and wait for the 9th Brigade landings. Unfortunately, those landings were delayed. The flotilla of Buffaloes navigating the Terneuzen canal had become stuck. Despite the best efforts of the engineers, who cut ramps in the canal bank to allow the Buffaloes to bypass the obstacle, H-hour – the hour at which an operation is scheduled to begin – had to be delayed until 0200 hours on 9 October. By then it was almost too late for 7th Brigade which came out of action 12 October after suffering 533 men killed and wounded and close to 200 cases of battle exhaustion. The value of their sacrifice in unlocking the defences of the Breskens Pocket is to be measured by the success of 9th Brigade's assault.

October 8th was a day of considerable tension; not only had the delay exposed 7th Brigade to an extra 24 hours of misery, there was understandable fear that the security of the amphibious assault would be compromised. One benefit of the delay was the recruitment of Lieutenant-Commander R.D. Franks, the naval liaison officer at Army Headquarters, to navigate the flotilla as the promised river pilots had not appeared. Shortly

Left: A Buffalo enters the water carrying Canadian troops destined for the Breskens Pocket.
LAC PA 131264

Below: Soldiers of the North Shore (New Brunswick) Regiment aboard a Buffalo LVT en route to Hoofdplaat, 11 October 1944.
LAC PA 138417

after midnight "the first LVT waddled down the ramp and splashed into the water." Lieutenant-Commander Franks recorded this description of the crossing:

> It was a nearly ideal night, calm and quiet with a half moon behind light cloud, but a bit of haze which restricted visibility to a mile at most. We were quite invisible from the north shore of the Scheldt, where all was quiet… Just as we cleared the land our artillery barrage started up, "plastering" the far beaches and other targets. The noise effectively blanketed our sounds and was generally most heartening. Our touch down was planned to be on either side of a groyne…we were able to identify it and then lie off flicking our lamps to guide the LVTs in. They deployed and thundered past us…I could see through my binoculars the infantry disembarking on dry land and form up and move off.…

The North Nova Scotia Regiment landing at Green Beach achieved complete surprise. To their left the Highland Light Infantry (HLI) was held up by the more extensive mud flats in which some Buffaloes bogged down. As well, their landing point, "Amber Beach," was much closer to the German positions at Biervliet, and the German response was far quicker.

While the North Novas and HLI established a beachhead, the Buffaloes returned to Terneuzen to transport the reserve battalion, the Stormont, Dundas and Glengarry Highlanders, plus the heavy mortars and machine guns of the Cameron Highlanders of Ottawa. They landed at "Green Beach," which was still not receiving much fire, at 1030 hours and moved off along the coast to capture Hoofdplaat. It was vitally important to expand the bridgehead as quickly as possible.

Field Marshal Walter Model's Army Group B Situation Report (sitrep) for 9 October described the German reaction:

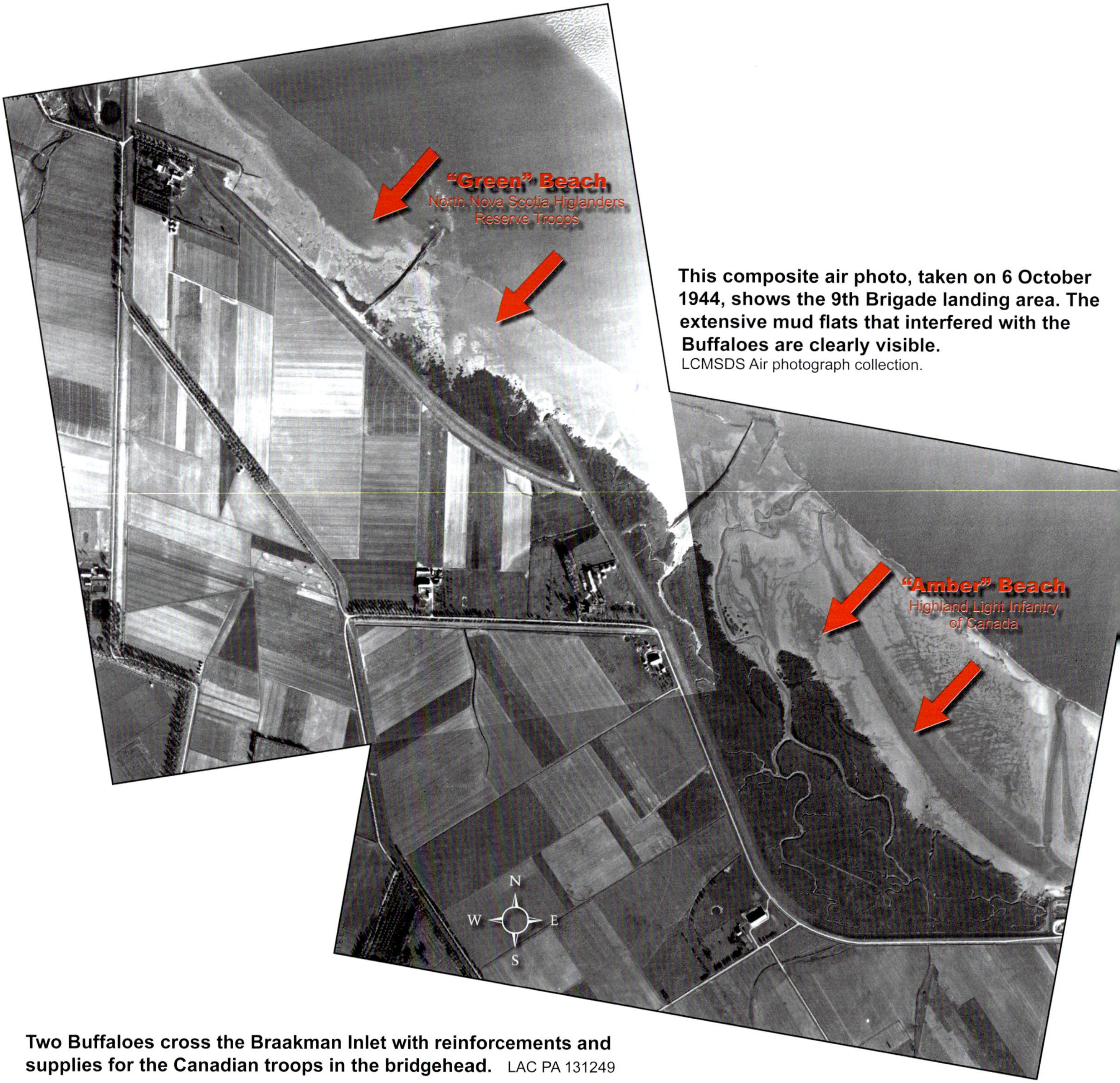

This composite air photo, taken on 6 October 1944, shows the 9th Brigade landing area. The extensive mud flats that interfered with the Buffaloes are clearly visible. LCMSDS Air photograph collection.

Two Buffaloes cross the Braakman Inlet with reinforcements and supplies for the Canadian troops in the bridgehead. LAC PA 131249

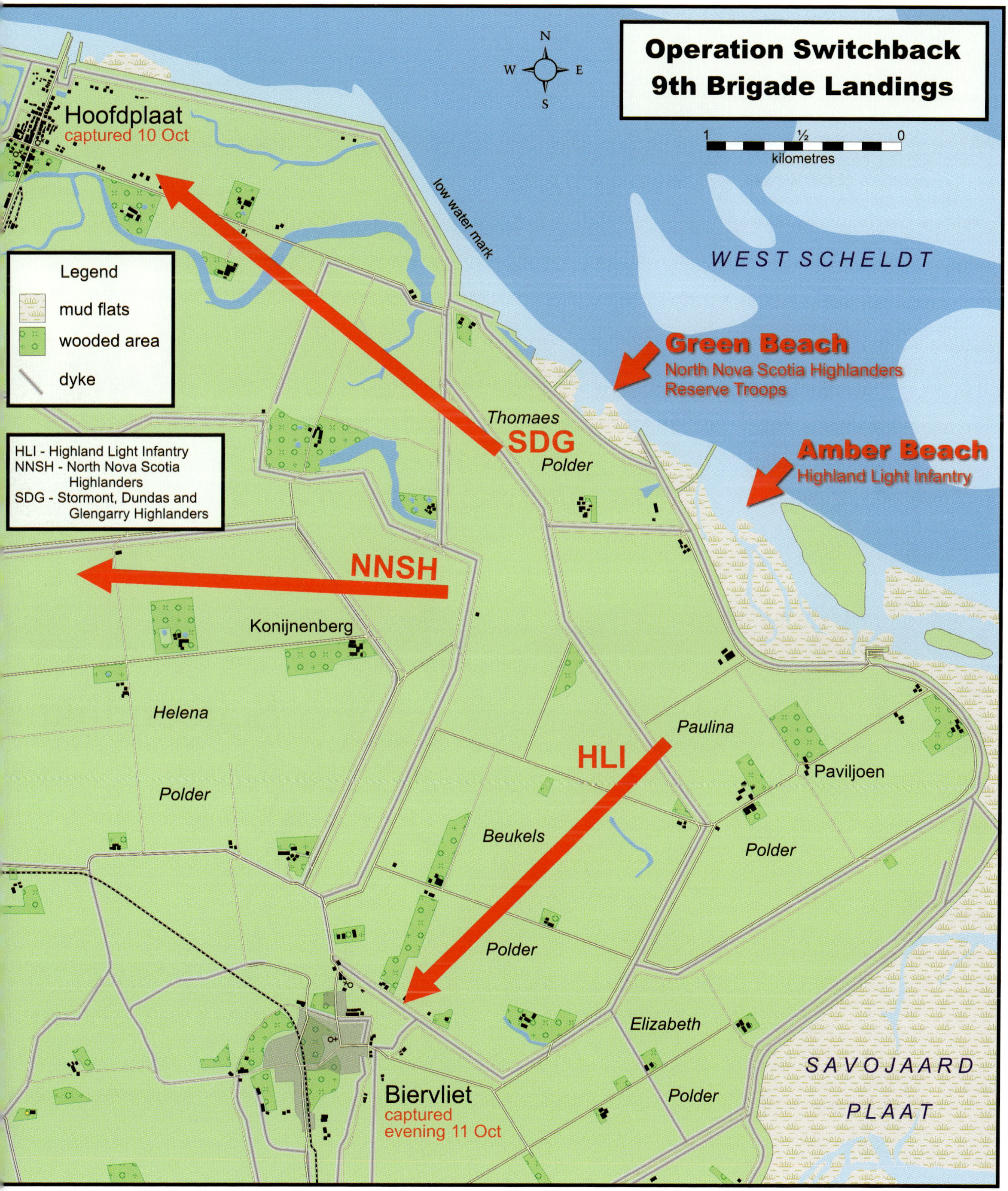

Operation Switchback
9th Brigade Landings
N
W
E
S
1
½
0
kilometres
Hoofdplaat
captured 10 Oct
low water mark
WEST SCHELDT
Legend
mud flats
wooded area
dyke
Green Beach
North Nova Scotia Highlanders
Reserve Troops
Thomaes
SDG
Polder
Amber Beach
Highland Light Infantry
HLI - Highland Light Infantry
NNSH - North Nova Scotia Highlanders
SDG - Stormont, Dundas and Glengarry Highlanders
NNSH
Konijnenberg
Helena
Polder
Paulina
HLI
Paviljoen
Beukels
Polder
Polder
Polder
Elizabeth
Polder
SAVOJAARD
PLAAT
Biervliet
captured evening 11 Oct

The battles fought in the Breskens pocket were ferocious. The effects of the fighting on the town of Schoondijke can be seen in the before and after air photos shown below. The capture of the town required hard fighting by the Highland Light Infantry on 22-23 October. The close-up map of Schoondijke at the bottom right is a detail from a 1944 defence overprint map. The red markings show expected German defences: x = wire; square box = concrete shelter; arrow head = machine gun; line with triangles = anti-tank ditch; cross with y-tail = anti-tank gun.

LCMSDS Air Photograph and Map Collection

18 October 1944▲

▼10 September 1944

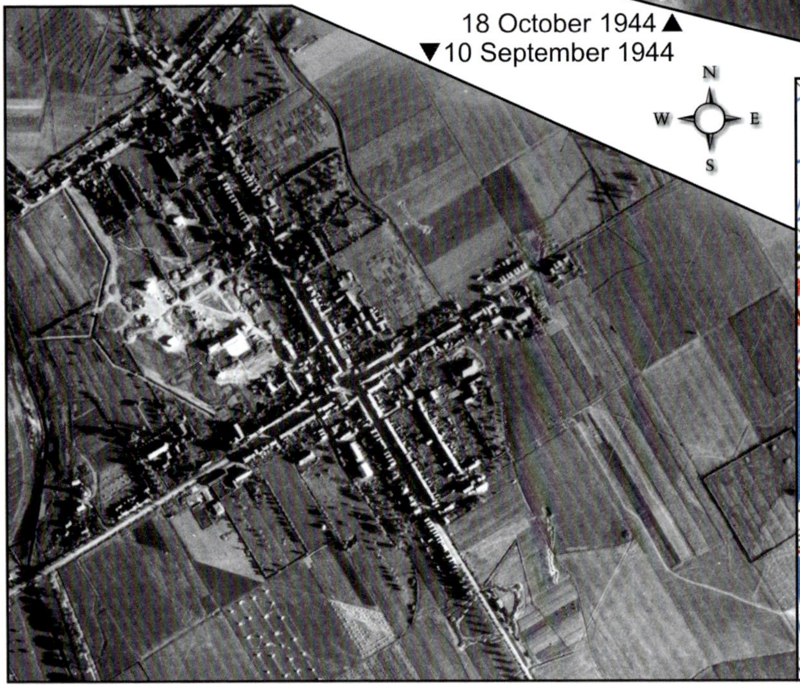

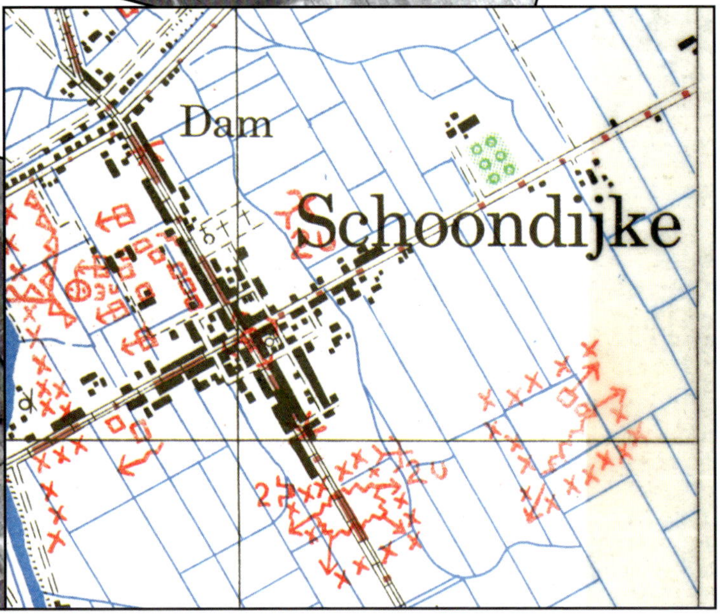

Today the enemy launched a decision-seeking attack on the Breskens bridgehead. While maintaining strong pressure against the southern front of 64th Inf. Division, he landed with four to five battalions and some tanks on the north-eastern tip establishing a new bridgehead 3 km deep and 6 km wide.

The German army had elevated the idea of immediate counterattacks into a battle doctrine which German commanders felt obligated to follow. Eberding had repeatedly attempted to evict 7th Brigade and now proposed to try the same tactics on 9th Brigade. Model's sitrep of 11 October stated: "At the new bridgehead German counterattacks were delayed by air attacks and

Bren gun carriers in soft, flooded ground beside a dyke in the Breskens Pocket, 28 October 1944.
LAC PA 131252

damaged roads. After finally getting under way at 1930 hours, they failed completely."

The complete and costly failure of these counterattacks was partly due to the combination of artillery barrages and tactical air power. On 11 October 84 Group reported, "Today the weather improved greatly and a new record was set for sorties [636] in direct support of the army." Fifteenth Field Regiment had moved forward to a position on the east side of the Braakman which allowed its gunners to "see their rounds falling."

The next morning bitter infantry battles erupted in a confused scene when both sides attempted to advance. It was at this point that the enormous flexibility of amphibious warfare proved decisive. Employing a smoke screen to mask the landing area Major-General Spry decided to land 8th Brigade in the north-eastern bridgehead. This was not an easy decision, for while the landing of the brigade could be readily accomplished, supplying three more battalions with a diminishing fleet of Buffaloes was no easy task. Spry was therefore forced to order 8th Brigade to attack due south to link up with 4th Division's infantry and open a land route into the pocket. Only then could both brigades move in strength to the west. General Eberding was later to tell Spry that the Canadians failed to exploit their opportunities,

A group from the Highland Light Infantry of Canada wait for the order to attack Breskens, 19 October 1944.
LAC PA 142104

particularly when they did not advance quickly into the centre of the pocket in the second week. After two "successful" surprise manoeuvres had cost his division upwards of 700 casualties, Spry may be forgiven for having preferred to do it step-by-step (dyke-by-dyke) with full logistical support. His decision may also have been influenced by divisional and corps intelligence officers who, after a month of extreme optimism, were now predicting a long, difficult battle. But the German counterattacks on the northeast bridgehead had not only failed to gain ground, they had exhausted the only reserves available. As 8th Brigade began its move from Biervliet, the Germans could do no more than delay the Canadian advance.

On 14 October Eberding entered into the spirit of National Socialism by issuing his own version of the infamous "kith and kin" law which ordered retaliation against the relatives of deserters:

> I hereby command that in cases where the names of deserters are ascertained their names will be made known to the civilian population at home and their next of kin will be looked upon as enemies of the German people... This order is to be read to all troops by 1500 hrs and reported, and as soon as read to all troops at once destroyed.

This was an empty gesture. The landing of the two Canadian brigades in the rear of the German positions doomed 64th Division. During the last two weeks of October German soldiers resisted until their positions were outflanked or taken under direct fire. Then the white flags would appear. More than 8,000 men surrendered to the Canadians before Eberding himself gave up and ordered the capitulation of Scheldt Fortress South on 2 November.

German soldiers, captured during the fighting in the Breskens Pocket, are escorted into captivity.
LAC PA 142103

The Tour

From Brugge you can easily visit the canal crossing battlefields of September and October 1944. To take them in chronological order drive to Moerbrugge where the Lincs, Argylls and SARs forced their way across the Gent canal. The community has created an interesting memorial sculpture made out of pieces of a Sherman tank. There is also a striking memorial "In grateful memory of our valiant liberators of the 10th Canadian Infantry Brigade" at Oostkamp.

At Moerkerke the tree-lined banks of the double canal line make this one of the most hauntingly beautiful battlefields you will encounter. The road on the south side of the canal is the Algonquinstraat. On the north side there is a memorial "In memory of the battle at Molentje 13-14 September 1944." Each year on the anniversary wooden crosses are placed here, one for each solder killed in action. Compare the ground to the air photo, and think about the task of the four Algonquin companies each of roughly 80 men. The attack was planned on the assumption that the enemy was not intending to

Right: A memorial to the 52 Canadians killed during the fighting at Moerbrugge and 12 locals killed during the occupation. The inscription on the memorial, contructed from the parts of a Sherman tank, says, "forging war into eternal peace."
Photo by J.A. Robertson

Below: Memorial to the Algonquin Regiment at Moerkerke. Each year on the annversary of the battle the locals place a wooden cross for each Canadian killed in the battle.
Photo by J.A. Robertson

Right: The Bison Memorial at the Canadabrug in Brugge. The inscription on the side states, "This bridge was erected in memory of the Canadian Forces who liberated the city of Bruges on Sepetmber the 12th 1944."
Photo by Linda Copp

hold the Breskens Pocket, an intelligence failure difficult to explain. Engineers were to bridge the canals quickly allowing the armour to cross into the bridgehead. Against a determined enemy and without armour the Algonquins stood little chance of success. The enemy infiltrated through to the dyke between the canals and the south bank before the operation was called off.

It will now be time to return to Brugge for a bit of relaxation, shopping or just a stroll around the town before dinner. There are several interesting memorials to visit in Brugge and the Canada Bridge (Canadabrug) is not too be missed. The west side of the bridge is flanked by two large bronze bison, the symbol of the Manitoba Dragoons who are credited with liberating the city. The Rileys entered the town at about the same time, but their role and the actions of the Lake Superior Regiment, which actually fought its way into Brugge before withdrawing, await recognition.

You will also want to visit the Canada Square (Canadaplein) where plaques on a low brick wall in a small park carry the inscription "To the memory

Right: The Canadian Military Cemetery at Adegem.

A view along the stretch of the Leopold Canal assaulted by 7th Canadian Infantry Brigade on 6 October 1944. This photo is taken from the N251 road bridge. The bunker (seen on page 39) is just behind the small tree on the left bank of the canal visible in the distance.

Above: Memorial to 7th Brigade in Eede.
Photo by Linda Copp

Above left: Memorial to 9th Brigade.

of the Canadian Heroes who died for liberty and civilization."

Begin your tour of the "Breskens Pocket" at the Canada Museum in Adegem. Once you reach the town signs will direct you to the site. This remarkable museum was created by a Gilbert van Landschoot who built the Canada Museum as a way of thanking Canadians for their role in the liberation of Belgium. His father, a member of the resistance, was saved from arrest by the Gestapo when the Canadians moved swiftly to secure the Adegem area. Mr. van Landschoot learned of this when his father was dying and since then much of his energy has been devoted to the Canada Museum. The marvellous stained glass panels with the badges of all Canadian regiments are just one of the impressive architectural details. The museum itself is devoted to the story of the occupation of Belgium and the liberation of the area in September and October 1944 by Canadian and Polish troops. The dioramas of Operation "Switchback" are particularly impressive <www.canadamuseum.be>.

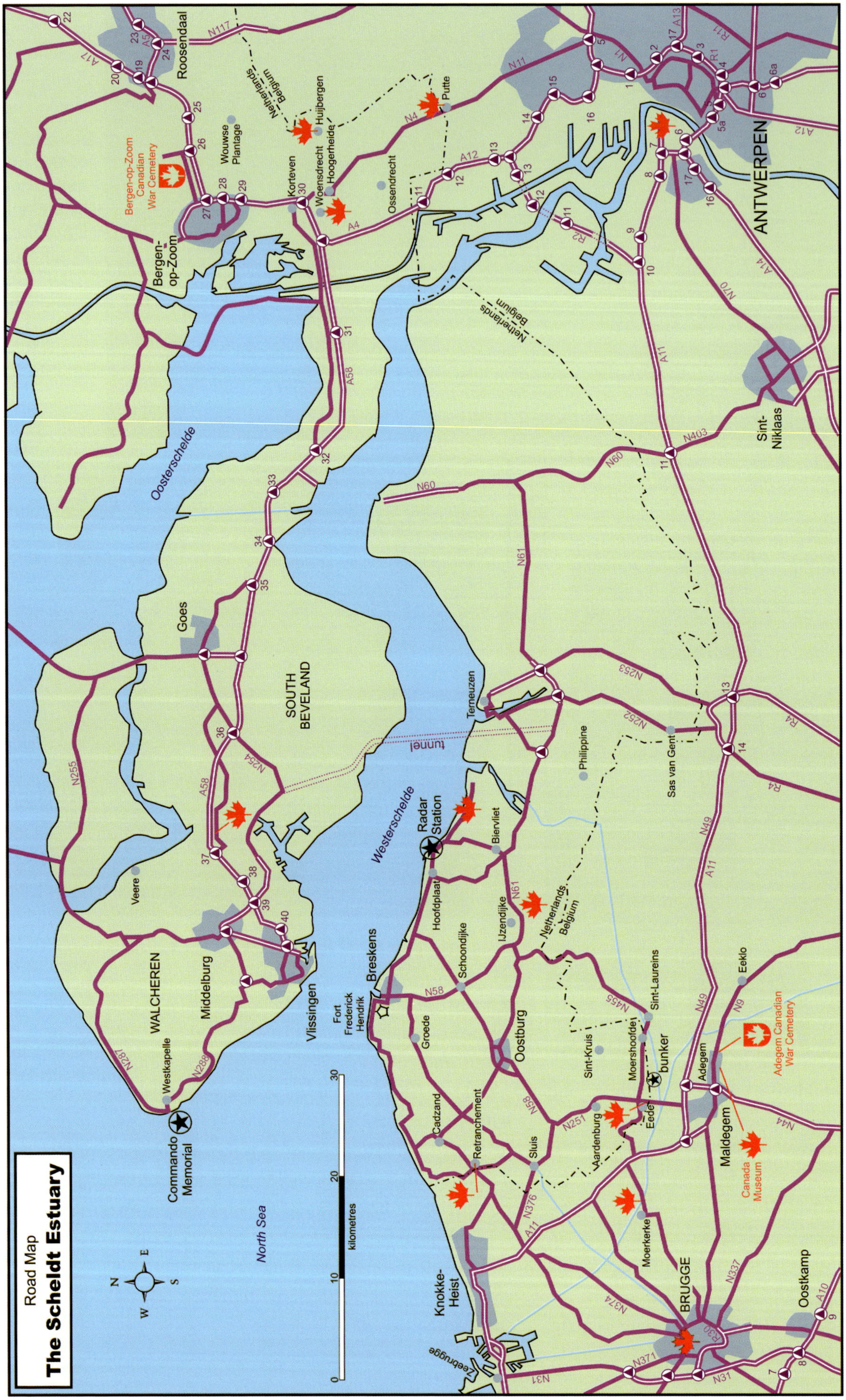
Road Map
The Scheldt Estuary
North Sea
kilometres
0 10 20 30
Commando Memorial
Westkapelle
WALCHEREN
Middelburg
Vlissingen
Veere
Oosterschelde
Goes
SOUTH BEVELAND
Westerschelde
Fort Frederick Hendrik
Breskens
Groede
Schoondijke
Hoofdplaat
Radar Station
Bierviet
IJzendijke
Netherlands
Belgium
Oostburg
Cadzand
Retranchement
Sluis
Aardenburg
Eede
Sint-Kruis
Moershoofde
bunker
Sint-Laureins
Philippine
Sas van Gent
Terneuzen
tunnel
Knokke-Heist
Zeebrugge
Moerkerke
BRUGGE
Oostkamp
Maldegem
Canada Museum
Adegem
Adegem Canadian War Cemetery
Eeklo
Sint-Niklaas
ANTWERPEN
Putte
Ossendrecht
Hoogerheide
Woensdrecht
Huijbergen
Korteven
Wouwse Plantage
Bergen-op-Zoom
Bergen-op-Zoom Canadian War Cemetery
Roosendaal

Mr. van Landschoot paid for the construction of the museum and the displays out of his own pocket but he was naturally anxious to cover the operating costs. He quickly learned that no military museum can possibly operate without a subsidy and decided to lure visitors by creating a series of magnificent gardens on the grounds adjacent to the museum. The gardens attract thousands of visitors many of whom then decide to visit the museum to learn, usually for the first time, about an important chapter in the history of Belgium and Canada. There is also a café on site.

Time your visit to Adegem to have an early lunch at the Museum and combine it with a visit to the Canadian Military Cemetery at Adegem which is just east of the town on the N9. There are 848 Canadians, largely from the 3rd Division, and 248 British and Polish graves here. The cemetery is a focal point for the annual commemoration of the liberation of the area in September.

To explore 7th "Western" Brigade's battlefield at the Leopold Canal, you should begin at the monument located at Eede just across the border in the Netherlands. The small square includes plaques recalling the Canadian contribution to the liberation of the area, the civilian victims "who did not live to see the liberation," and the return of Queen Wilhelmina who crossing into the Netherlands here in March 1945 after four years and ten months of exile. Her daughter, the future Queen Juliana and her children were guests of the Canadian people in Ottawa during the war.

Drive east on the Briversweg Road towards Sint Laureins, re-entering Belgium, and turning right before you cross the Leopold Canal to reach the Bailey Bridge constructed by the Royal Canadian Engineers in 1944. The plaque placed on the approach to the bridge by the village of Sint Laureins commemorates all those involved in the liberation of the area and especially the men of the Canadian Scottish Regiment who attacked across the canal here on 6 October 1944. Return to the Briversweg and follow it to the hamlets of Moershoofd and Oosthoek liberated by the Canscots. Back at the Breskens highway, the N251 turn south (left) and park by the canal. The road along the north bank of the canal is for bikes and pedestrians only so unless you absolutely need to

One of the many detailed dioramas at the Canada Museum in Adegem. This scene show a mortar team from 3rd Division preparing a shoot over the Leopold Canal.
Photo by Christopher R. Evans

drive please walk the few hundred metres to the large pillbox which dominated the assault area where the Regina and Royal Montreal Regiment companies crossed the Leopold. You will have no difficulty in understanding the challenge confronting the Canadians who fought here.

The next stage of your journey involves driving north to Schoondijke in the heart of the Breskens Pocket. The N58 turns north to Breskens but you should continue northeast to Sasput, the coast road and Hoofdplaat. The memorial to the 9th Brigade which carried out the highly successful assault landing in this area is to the east of Hoofdplaat.

To visit the actual beaches where the 9th Brigade came ashore return along the coast road to a parking area opposite the modern radar tower. Park and climb the dyke. The North Nova Scotia Regiment's "Green" Beach was west (left) of the groyne, while "Amber" Beach, the Highland Light Infantry landing area, was just to the east of it. The shoreline has changed little since 1944 and the groyne remains a recognizable marker.

The Glens advanced from the beachhead to Hoofdplaat. Follow the coastal road to the village where a simple lunch or picnic supplies can be obtained. There is a marker here for the starting point of the Hoofdplaat to Knokke-Heist Canadian Liberation March which begins here on 1 November every year. Hundreds of young, and not-so-young, Dutch and Belgium citizens walk 33 kilometres, retracing the path of the Canadian troops who liberated the region. The route, a kind of compromise between the paths of 8th and 9th Brigades, goes from Hoofdplaat to Oostburg by back roads, then on to Zuidzande, Retranchement, Oosthoek and ends at Canada Square in Knokke-Heist. For information, contact Danny Lannoy, "Canadian Liberation March" (dannylannoy@knokkeheist.be).

From Hoofdplaat 9th Brigade advanced towards Breskens with the Glens on the coastal flank and the North Novas to their right. It took a week of intense combat for each polder before the enemy withdrew to a new defensive line. 8th Brigade, which started west from Biervliet, found Ijzendijke well defended on the 15th but abandoned the next day.

The battle for Breskens involved the use of enough artillery and air power to virtually level the town. The Glens had to deal with pockets of the enemy and the North Novas had initial problems persuading the garrison of Fort Frederik Hendrik

"Green" Beach as it appears today from the top of the dyke. The groyne separating "Green" and "Amber" Beaches is visible at the right, as are the extensive mud flats at low tide.

to give up but in the end they too joined the more than 3,000 German soldiers who had surrendered. On the 20th, the HLI fought their way into Schoondijke. The next day they turned the northern sector over to 7th Brigade which, after five days of rest, was judged ready to go back into action.

The battle for Oostburg began on 24 October with the Chaudières in the lead. The QORs took over working their way forward along the banks of the Groote Gat. It took another day to clear the last holdouts in Oostburg. In the meantime, 7th Brigade

Before (3 September 1944) and after (18 October 1944) air photos of Fort Frederik Hendrik. Despite the damage from bombs and shells the garrison of the fort held out until 25 October 1944.
LAC C 105855 & LCMSDS Air Photo Collection 223/4031

The Ijzendijke Explosion

On the night of 19 October 1944, Churchill AVREs from 284 Armoured Assault Squadron Royal Engineers, part of 79th Armoured Division, made camp at a farm near Ijzendijke, the Netherlands. In the morning the tank crews prepared for an assault that would take place the next day. Just before noon a convoy of Canadian trucks arrived from the 7th Canadian Infantry Brigade Company, Royal Canadian Army Service Corps, with provisions for the tank unit. In addition to the regular rations, supplies, petrol and ammunition, one lorry carried a cargo of some three tons of liquid nitroglycerine. This highly unstable explosive was for the "Conger," a bren carrier adapted to launch a flexible hose across a minefield. The liquid explosive was then pumped into the hose and detonated to breach the minefield.

At approximately 1300 hours a huge explosion rocked the field. The cause of the explosion is unknown, but the result was devastating. A total of 41 men, British and Canadian, were killed and over 50 others wounded, many seriously. Ten armoured vehicles were destroyed and it would be over a month before the squadron was again committed to operations.

Fifty years after the tragedy, Martin Reagan, a Churchill AVRE tank commander who survived the explosion, returned to the site for the first time since the war. His visit set in motion a series of events which culminated with the dedication of a memorial at the site on 20 October 1997.

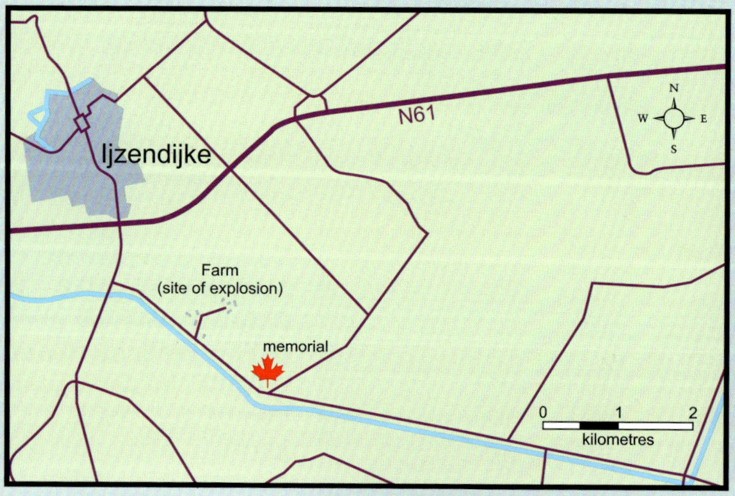

Below right: A closeup of the memorial taken at the dedication ceremony on 20 October 1997.

Bottom: The monument honouring the victims of the explosion at the farm near Ijzendijke on 20 October 1944. The farm is visible in the background.

This public relations photo carries the following original caption: "The crew of a Canadian anti-tank gun hail one of their countrymen as he passes while touring the ruins of Breskens after the port had fallen to Canadian forces, 29 October 1944."

had reached the coast north of Cadzand-Bad. The enemy withdrew to Retranchement and Sluis. 9th Brigade took over for the final offensive into Knokke-Heist. There is a small museum in Oostburg that pays tribute to the Canadian role in liberating the Breskens area – Museum Switchback. The museum, located in the centre of Oostburg, is open Saturdays in June, July and August from 1 to 5 pm. It is also open by appointment. <www. switchback40-45.tk>

Continue on the coast road into Breskens. There is a memorial to the civilians who died in the fighting for Breskens just off the Scheldekade on the east side of the town. Otherwise the citizens of Breskens prefer to forget the fury of war unleashed against their town in 1944. Fort Frederik Hendrik has been transformed into a camping ground and trailer park. Some of the characteristic fortress-shape can be seen in parts of the moat now used for recreation. View it from the top of the dyke.

Most of the Dutch towns in Zeeland were badly damaged in the month-long battle and apart from some bunkers around Breskens there is little to see that can be related to October 1944. Groede was the site of a military hospital and Canadian artillery did not target the village even after the Reginas insisted that the Church tower was being used to direct fire on their advance. Cadzand-Bad, a small beach resort liberated by the Canadian Scottish, is pleasant for lunch. Retranchement has an important monument on the west side of the village. The plaque beside "Hickmanbrug" reads:

> After the offensive of the Westerschelde the Canadians fought an exhaustive battle in the polders of Zeeuwsch-Vlaamse along the dikes in the direction of the Belgium border, and Knokke-Heist. At the end of October, the Royal Canadian Engineer Regiment under the leadership of Sergeant J.L. Hickman reached

An air photo taken on 8 October 1944 showing the town of Groede. A number of buildings can be seen prominently displaying the red cross on their rooftops.
LCMSDS Air Photo 228/3008

the drainage canal at Retranchement. Under heavy shellfire, they erected a Bailey bridge on this site on 31 October 1944 where Sgt. Hickman was mortally wounded. In tribute to him and his comrades this bridge was dedicated in his name on 30 October 1989. This simple monument has been adopted by the children of the local school.

From Retranchement it is a short drive to Knokke-Heist. There is a monument to the liberators of Knokke-Heist in the Versetplein (Resistance) Square. It includes the badges of the three Highland Regiments of 9th Brigade. Knokke-Heist is a major Belgian seaside resort so summer traffic is very heavy. Be sure and visit the new (2009) "For Freedom Museum" on Ramskapellestraat <www.forfreedommuseum.be>. Zeebrugge, the last town to be liberated in Flanders, is a busy ferry port. Return to Brugge on the N31 or take the time to drive the coastal road, the N34 to Ostend, where a large intact section of the "Atlantic Wall" has been preserved <http://users.telenet.be/alex.deseyne/ENG/AtlantikwallE.htm>

Hickman Bridge in Retranchement
Photo by J.A. Robertson

North From Antwerp: Woensdrecht, Walcheren, Bergen-op-Zoom

Sherman tank monument at Westkapelle on Walcheren Island.

Operation "Market Garden," Montgomery's great gamble, required the support of all available elements of Second British Army. He, therefore, assigned the holding operation at Antwerp to First Canadian Army. On 15 September the Dunkirk perimeter was handed over to the 4th Special Service Brigade and 2nd Canadian Infantry Division began its move to Antwerp.

The Belgian White Brigade had played a crucial role in securing the city and its vital docks for the Allies. Eugene Colson, a merchant navy officer and resistance leader, had led his men into the dock area and, with the arrival of the British, urged an assault on Merxem, the industrial suburb north of the Albert Canal. The British had no orders to move north from Antwerp and the best they would attempt was a three-company crossing of the Albert Canal which was withdrawn after suffering 150 casualties. The next day, 6 September, the bulk of the British forces left Antwerp in preparation for Montgomery's attempt to bounce the Rhine.

Antwerp was a strange place in September 1944. The civilian population was caught up in the euphoria of liberation and seemed almost oblivious to the presence of the Germans in the northern suburbs of the city. Some civilians went about their affairs to the point of crossing back and forth over the Albert Canal from the German to the Allied sector. The Belgian resistance, on the other hand, was active in attempting to extend the dock area perimeter. The Essex Scottish and the Royal Hamilton Light Infantry took over the dock defences and on the night of 20 September the Essex were hard hit by a German attack which was apparently intended to seize and destroy a railway bridge. Heavy fighting raged throughout the night but the enemy was beaten off.

The area around the 4th Brigade positions had been flooded by the Germans until White Brigade patrols supported by Canadian artillery

Senior officers of the Belgian White Brigade lead a parade through the port area of Antwerp to honour their fallen comrades, October 1944. Eugene Colson (far right) was responsible for leading his unit to secure the Antwerp dockyards to prevent their destruction by the Germans.

secured the sluice gates, allowing the tidal water to be drained. The RHLI moved its lines forward to protect this site on 22 September. From that date until 2 October, no major initiative was taken by either side.

On 18 September, 5th Brigade made the trek to Antwerp taking up positions along the Albert Canal near Wijnegem. Its orders were to begin the advance north from Antwerp "with the resources available." Once again the Canadians were warned not to incur heavy losses. At a Brigade Orders Group the Black Watch was told to place scouts (and if possible a patrol) across the canal to determine the extent of German resistance. It was not difficult to establish that the Germans were indeed resisting and the Calgary Highlanders were ordered to prepare a full battalion attack which succeeded brilliantly.

Sixth Brigade was ordered to seize a strong bridgehead across the Turnhout Canal on 24 September. Les Fusiliers Mont-Royal made a virtually unopposed crossing at Lochtenberg but were severely counterattacked. The South Saskatchewans were also able to cross and cling to a narrow foothold on the north bank of the canal for a few hours but artillery and mortar fire made bridging impossible and the troops were withdrawn that night.

In the meantime, 49th (West Riding) Division had crossed the canal at Turnhout, so 2nd Division was able to turn the German position from the northeast. The FMRs led off on the morning of the 28th. The Black Watch attacked St. Leonard that night, and, at a cost of 94 casualties, the town was captured. Brecht was taken the next day.

Interrogation reports of German officers who commanded units opposed to 2nd Division suggest that the bitter fighting of the last days of September forced 67th Corps to commit all available resources to try and prevent this flanking manoeuvre.

German sources describe these units as anything but first-class fighting formations and endlessly bemoan the equipment and ammunition shortages which further limited their effectiveness. Nevertheless, each of the three German divisions had deployed between six and eight thousand men and, in the circumstances of the period, a very high percentage of them were used as combat troops.

Meanwhile, in Merxem, the northern suburb of Antwerp, the Belgian White Brigade was rushing to harass a withdrawing enemy. On 2 October 4th Brigade moved into the suburb and

British and American flags fly over the city of Antwerp, 26 September 1944. The Scheldt River is visible bisecting the photograph.
LAC PA 137317

the next day the Essex Scottish pushed forward to Fort de Merxem and Shooten taking batches of prisoners from the 70th Infantry Division.

Hundreds of German soldiers had surrendered in the first days of October, and now with the canal defences broken the enemy appeared to be in full retreat. Divisional intelligence reported "definite indications of enemy withdrawal" and noted that prisoners were from a wide variety of units and included many low-category personnel. The main enemy force barring the route forward was thought to be the 70th German Infantry Division, an unusual unit made up of men who suffered from ulcers.

Woensdrecht

Back at Corps headquarters the same optimism prevailed. The Intelligence Summary for 7 October boldly insisted that the enemy had "given up any plan he might have had to stand on the approach to Walcheren." Despite Ultra, Allied intelligence had still failed to grasp German intentions. On the same day that 2nd Canadian Corps distributed its appreciation, General Gustav von Zangen issued an order which declared that "the defence of the approaches to Antwerp represents a task which is decisive for the further conduct of the war." Von Zangen did not just offer words, he ordered his army reserve, "Battlegroup Chill," including the 6th Parachute Regiment, to Woensdrecht with orders to bar access to Beveland and Walcheren.

Lieutenant-General Erich Diestel, commander of the mixed bag of divisional fragments defending the area north of Antwerp, described the arrival of the reinforcements when he was interviewed in 1945:

> On 2 October the Canadians attacked north from Merxem and in three days had driven the

division's right flank back to Putte, a distance of some 7 kms...There was no regular line to hold at this time, but rather a series of tactical points...The division had lost over 800 men in the battle for the Turnhout and Albert Canals and was in a very tired state. About 7 October, in almost melodramatic fashion, aid came in the form of the 15th Army Assault Battalion consisting of about 1000 men from the Army Battle School and the Von der Heydte Parachute Regiment of about 2500 fanatical and eager young parachutists.

The Canadians did not learn of von Zangen's decision until the German reinforcements arrived, but the Acting Corps Commander, Major-General Charles Foulkes, and the Acting Divisional Commander, Brigadier R H. Keefler, were well aware that the division was running a great risk by moving north with an unprotected eastern flank. Keefler decided to commit 6th Brigade and most of the one understrength armoured regiment available, the Fort Garry Horse, to protect that sector. This meant that only two brigades with one squadron of tanks were available to push on to the villages of Ossendrecht, Huijbergen, Hoogerheide and Woensdrecht.

On the morning of 7 October the Calgary Highlanders took over the lead. They had been briefed to work within an elaborate artillery fire plan that assigned code names to a large number of pre-arranged targets. Instead of relying on a creeping barrage, the company commanders, through the FOO, called down fire and when satisfied, "simply lifted artillery to other positions and watched results." The Calgaries spent most of the day working forward to Hoogerheide by this method.

Dutch civilians and air reconnaissance had provided fairly detailed information on the arrival of major German reinforcements and both division and corps intelligence accepted an estimate of between 2,000 and 3,000 troops. Brigadier Keefler reacted to this information by ordering 4th and 5th

A 25-pounder of 2nd Canadian Infantry Division firing on German targets north of Antwerp from the bank of the Scheldt river, 2 October 1944.
LAC PA 131239

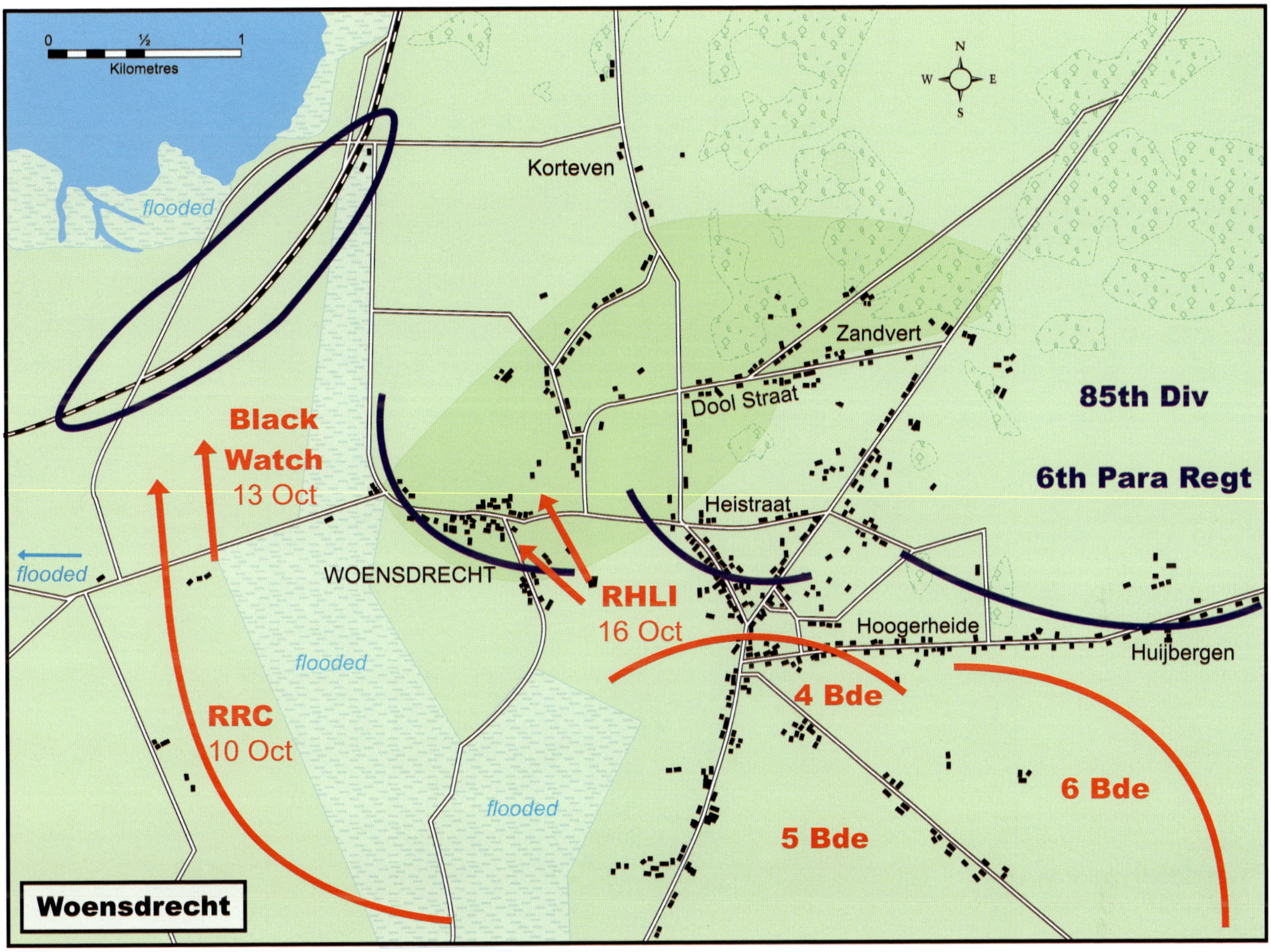

Brigades to go over to the defensive and prepare for a major attack which the Army intelligence section, probably on the basis of Ultra decrypts, had predicted for the night of the 8th.

The German attack began with intermittent mortaring and shelling which seemed designed to cover the infiltration of patrols. The Black Watch captured one group of 24 young soldiers. The War Diary notes that they belonged to parachute battalions, ranged in age from 20 to 26, and were "fine physical specimens, keen to fight and with excellent morale." Their high morale had not prevented them from advancing into a trap, suggesting that inexperience and overconfidence were also characteristics of the parachutists.

By mid-day of the 10th the German counterattack seemed to be spent. Von der Heydte's regiment had suffered heavy casualties, estimated at 480 men, in addition to more than 50 prisoners of war. Much is made in the secondary literature of the prowess of the German officer corps and the fighting power of the German infantry. Yet the battle for Hoogerheide demonstrated major deficiencies in German tactics which was not uncommon in Northwest Europe. Von der Heydte had launched a frontal attack against forces which had gone over to the defensive. He persisted in pressing forward despite heavy losses. To attack in this manner, when reconnaissance would have shown the weakness of the Canadian right flank, suggests overconfidence and doctrinal rigidity. The battle also indicates that both in their defensive positions and in their tactical counterattacks the Canadians were more than a match for the enemy.

Two Dutch children supervise while crewmen from the Fort Garry Horse repair the track of their Sherman "Firefly." Putte, Netherlands, 6 October 1944.
LAC PA 137140

On the evening of 10 October 5th Brigade was pulled back into reserve with orders to prepare for another attempt to seal off the Beveland Isthmus. The Acting Corps Commander had arrived at Divisional Headquarters during some of the heaviest fighting on the 9th with new instructions for offensive action. Foulkes informed Keefler that the South Alberta Regiment would come under his command, to help protect the still vulnerable flank. Other 4th Division units were promised later that week. Several new plans were developed but the events of the next few days were probably determined by the unexpected success of a company of the Royal Regiment of Canada, "which forced its way forward through the difficult polderland between Woensdrecht and the coast to reach the embankment carrying the railway from Beveland to the mainland." The next day, 11 October, the Germans struck all across the front in a renewed attempt to overwhelm the Canadians. Since Foulkes had ordered 4th Brigade, with both the Maisonneuves and South

Sasks under command to maintain pressure, 4th Brigade and the 6th Parachute Regiment flailed away at each other throughout the day. The Royal Regiment fought off six separate counterattacks – "No ground was given and heavy casualties inflicted" – but its own attempt to hold the railway embankment was beaten back. The RHLI and South Sasks improved their positions in the Hoogerheide-Huijbergen area, but movement attracted well-placed mortar fire and no serious advance was attempted.

Foulkes met with Keefler that night and outlined a plan which called for 5th Brigade "to plug the neck" of the isthmus by attacking through the Royal Regiment of Canada position. One battalion would seize the railway embankment, the other two would then go through to seal the approaches to Beveland. Brigadier W.J. Megill, commanding 5th Brigade, protested that the enemy forces in the area were too strong and too well dug-in. The terrain, he insisted, offered the defender too many advantages. His battalions, which had now been in constant action for two weeks, had lost a large number of experienced officers, NCOs and men, and there had been no time to integrate the reinforcements. Foulkes had heard all of this before and his only concession was to promise that the attack would have all available support, including whatever ammunition the artillery and mortar units required. Fifth Brigade was given 24 hours to prepare.

Foulkes had little choice in the matter. On 9 October Field Marshal Montgomery had issued a directive which emphasized offensive action by Second British Army in the Nijmegen sector. First Canadian Army was told to use "all available resources on the operations designed to give us free use of the port of Antwerp," but only 2nd and 3rd Divisions were immediately available. Montgomery did promise reinforcements. The 104th US and the 52nd (Lowland) Scottish Divisions would both be allotted to Simonds, but neither would be available for at least ten days. There could be no question of waiting for these substantial reinforcements, and the Canadians would have to get on as best they could.

When Eisenhower received a copy of Montgomery's directive he had on his desk a report from Admiral Bertram Ramsay, the Allied naval commander, which criticized the pace of operations to clear the Scheldt and noted that the Canadians were being handicapped by an ammunition shortage. Eisenhower, unhappy with Montgomery's conduct of operations, used this information in a message to Monty which concluded, "I must emphasize that of all our operations on our entire front from Switzerland to the Channel, I consider Antwerp of first importance and I believe that the operations to clear up the entrance require your personal attention." Montgomery was furious at this reprimand, accusing Ramsay of "wild statements" and denied that there was an ammunition shortage. The Field Marshal also insisted that Eisenhower had agreed to his policy of making the "main effort" against the Ruhr.

The most important immediate effect of this high-level confrontation was to put enormous pressure on the two Canadian infantry divisions. On the night of 9 October, 2nd Division was informed that "the limit to artillery ammunition expenditure [which Monty had denied existed] has been removed." The battle was to be continued with new intensity and there was little that any Canadian commander could do about it. When, on the night of 11 October, Foulkes allowed Megill to postpone the brigade's attack until the 13th he went about as far as he could go.

The extra 24 hours were put to good use. The first phase of the assault, code-named Operation "Angus," would be undertaken by the Black Watch as the Maisonneuves were still more than 200 riflemen short and the Calgaries had borne the brunt of the fighting at Hoogerheide. The attack was built around an elaborate scheme to shoot the battalion on to the dyke, one company at a time. One medium and two field regiments, as well as the heavy mortars and machine guns of

This air photo, taken on 6 October 1944, shows the area attacked by The Black Watch (Royal Highland Regiment) of Canada on "Black Friday" – 13 October 1944.

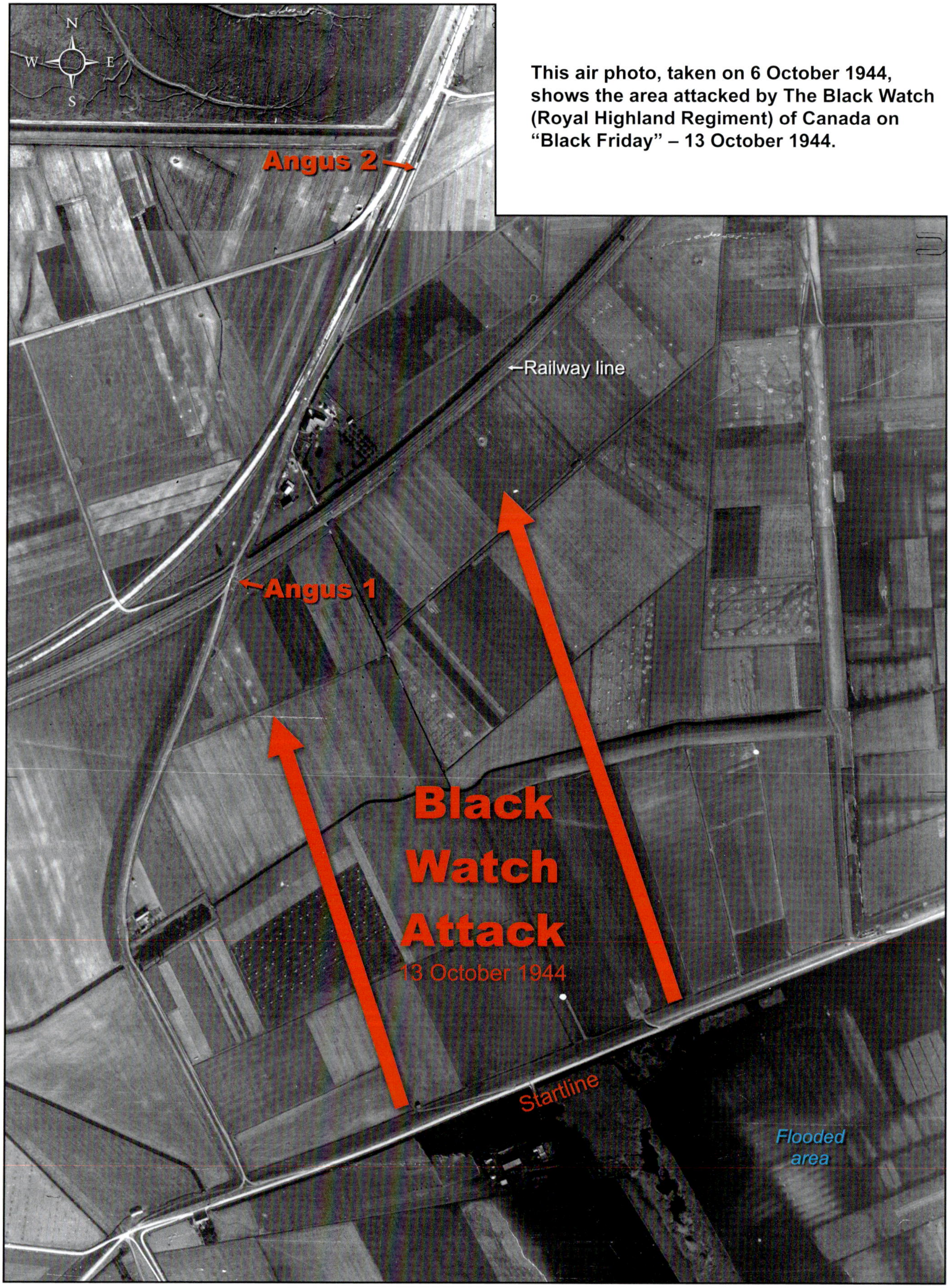

the Toronto Scottish, would provide the basic firepower. A Royal Marine heavy anti-aircraft regiment with 3.7-inch guns was also available but it was short of ammunition. The Fort Garry Horse supplied a troop of tanks but, given the field of fire available to enemy anti-tank guns, it could be used only to provide an initial shoot on the dyke junction, code-named "Angus 1." The Spitfires and Typhoons of 84 Group would also participate, weather permitting.

For the Black Watch 13 October was "Black Friday," the second single-day disaster in the history of the Royal Highland Regiment of Canada. It was not so much total casualties, 145, but the ratio of dead-to-wounded that marked the day's fighting. Fifty-six Black Watch soldiers were killed or died of wounds and 27 were taken prisoner.

The post-mortems on this engagement began almost immediately. Lieutenant William Shea, the battalion intelligence officer who had watched the battle unfold from an observation post, suggests that there were three reasons for the failure of the RHC attacks, "first, the great natural defensive strength of the obstacles attacked; second, the determined opposition of the enemy who were paratroops; third, and most important, the poor quality of reinforcements received by the battalion." Shea's observations are but one example of complaints about reinforcements from 2nd Division units in October. With the Minister of National Defence, J.L. Ralston, visiting Corps and Divisional Headquarters amidst rumours of the possible dispatch of conscripts from Canada for active service, it was natural that hard-pressed infantry officers would seize on this explanation,

This modern air photo shows the area north of Woensdrecht attacked by the Black Watch (Royal Highland Regiment) of Canada on "Black Friday" – 13 October 1944. The terrain has been changed substantially by the new highways (A58 & A4) bisecting the battlefield.
Photo by Evert Stieber

Right: Funeral for Black Watch soldiers killed around Woensdrecht, October 1944.
LCMSDS Photo Collection

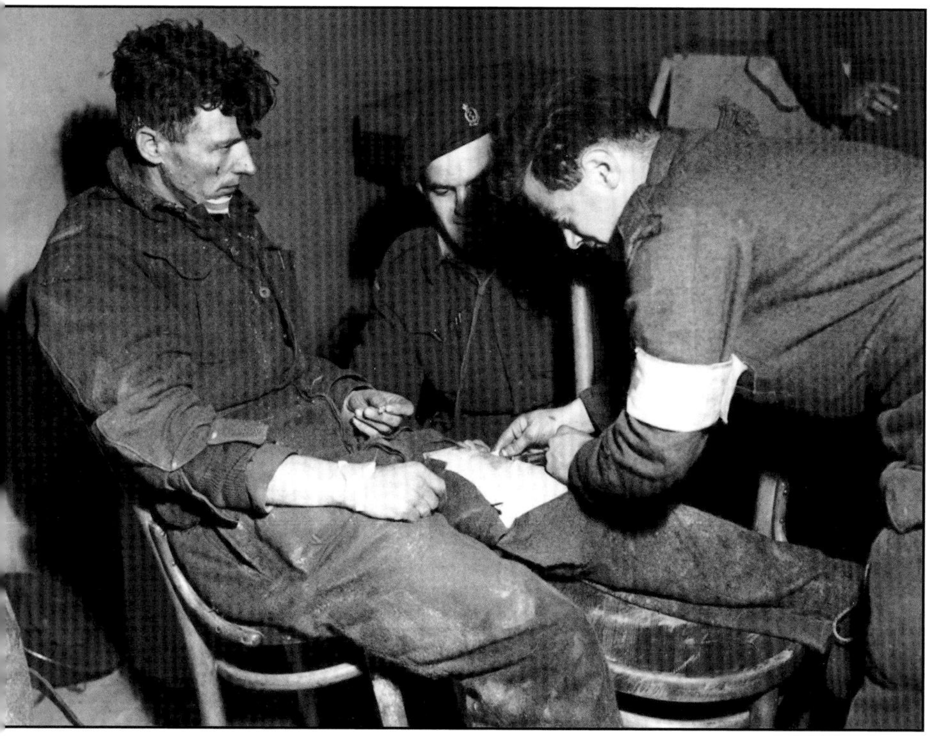

Below: The stress of battle clearly shows on the face of Private W.R.Van Herne, Calgary Highlanders, as he has his wounds attended to by medical personnel.
LAC PA 131260

but no one who studies the battle closely will believe that any battalion could have captured this position on its own.

The Black Watch were not the only Canadian unit to suffer from Montgomery's hesitation in assigning priority to Antwerp. Despite a series of sharp counterattacks on the South Sasks at Hoogerheide the weekend was spent preparing for the Royal Hamilton Light Infantry to assault Woensdrecht and the low ridge behind the village. The RHLI attack on 16 October was initially successful, as the Germans withdrew from the village when the barrage began. All four companies were dug in when the inevitable counterattacks began. For the next four days the RHLI defended the village in an action which cost them 167 casualties. Companies from the Essex Scottish and Maisonneuves were also drawn into the battle as 6th Parachute Regiment attacked repeatedly despite its own mounting losses.

On 16 October the War Diarist at 5th Brigade headquarters recorded a view shared by everyone in 2nd Division: "Cannot understand why they do not put more troops in the area and finish the job once and for all instead of playing about, shifting first one battalion and then the other. This is beginning to look like a winter campaign unless something breaks soon." Help was on the way. As the battle for Woensdrecht raged, Montgomery finally agreed to assign "complete priority" to operations to open Antwerp.

The official Canadian historian, C.P. Stacey, has noted, "As soon as the new orders took effect the situation north of Antwerp was transformed. The 4th Canadian Armoured Division...was to be used as a hammer to loosen the German formations confronting 2nd Division." Fourth Division was to clear the country northeast of Woensdrecht and free 2nd Division's flank. It in turn would be supported by 49th West Riding, 1st Polish Armoured and 104th US "Timberwolf" Division in an operation which was certain to force a rapid German retreat to the Maas.

Beveland and Walcheren Island

Second Division staff now turned their attention to Beveland and the approaches to Walcheren Island. Operation "Vitality I" was launched on the morning of the 24th. In the early hours of "a rainy, pitch-bleak morning two 'Jock Columns' of Essex Regiment Infantry, 8 Recce Armoured Cars, and Fort Garry tanks" set out for the Beveland Canal. Progress was slow and when three recce cars and three tanks were knocked out the armoured thrust ended. The next day, a conventional infantry attack with the artillery pouring fire on two crossroads brought complete success. That night "Vitality II," an amphibious assault across the Scheldt, carried out by a brigade of the 52nd (Lowland) Division, forced the enemy to abandon their new defensive line at the Beveland Canal and conduct a hasty retreat to Walcheren. The Scots, their advance slowed by mud, mines and the natural caution of green troops, failed to prevent this exodus. The 52nd, trained initially as an elite mountain unit and then converted to a specialized "air transportable" division, was not happy with its new assignment in land below sea level.

The Canadians found their new partners more than a little strange. An officer of the Royal Regiment of Canada left an account of his first meeting with the Scots which has become a classic Canadian military anecdote:

> In the early hours of the 29th I was out with a unit of carriers, maintaining a standing patrol on the left flank of the battalion. In order to complete our patrol, we utilized some Dutch bicycles to patrol down a dyke to the bank of the West Scheldt. All our men were desperately tired and in a filthy, wet, muddy condition. On our way we were terribly surprised to find a party of what were obviously Allied troops landing in a small boat. Then forth from the boat onto the shore stepped what seemed to me to be the finest soldier I had ever seen in my life, a fine figure of a Scottish gentleman, carrying the shepherd's crook affected by some senior Scottish officers in place of a cane or a swagger stick. He had a small pack neatly adjusted on his back. (I had absolutely no idea

A truck belonging to a medical unit crosses a pontoon bridge over the Beveland Canal.
LAC PA 138427

Two Canadian soldiers examine a concealed German anti-tank gun position on the dyke overlooking the Walcheren Causeway.
LAC PA 131254

where mine was and couldn't care less.) His gas cape, was neatly rolled. (I had last seen mine somewhere around Eterville.) He had his pistol in a neatly blanched web holster. (I had mine in my hip pocket.) He had a neatly kept map case. (I had mine stuck in my breast pocket.) He was a Colonel and I was a Captain. His boots were neatly polished and I was wearing turned-down rubber boots. I did manage to salute, although I think it must have been haphazard. He politely enquired if we were Canadians. (Although who else could have looked as we did?) I assured him we were. He asked if I could direct him to battalion headquarters. I did better than that. I escorted him to battalion headquarters. I was taking no chances on losing such a beautiful specimen to the German Army.

* * * * *

Sixth Brigade took over the advance using all three battalions to break across the Beveland Canal. The South Sasks improvised a route using part of the damaged railway bridge. The Queen's Own Cameron Highlanders kept to the coast of the Oosterschelde (East Scheldt) liberating Wemeldinge. Eighth Recce Regiment advanced through the Camerons and one squadron ferried its armoured cars over to the island of North Beveland where 450 enemy were taken prisoner.

To the south the Essex Scottish had advanced all the way to the west shore of Beveland. The Acting Divisional Commander, Brigadier Keefler, responding to the constant pressure from Corps Headquarters, "asked" Brigadier F.N. Cabeldu, commander of 4th Brigade, "to try and exploit further and push a bridgehead over the causeway." Cabeldu protested, arguing that only very fresh troops could accomplish the task. The alternative, a

The German view of the Walcheren Causeway, looking towards Beveland and the direction of the Canadian attack. Photograph taken in 1946.
CFJIC PMR 82-078

proper assault crossing of the water obstacle, would require some time to mount. Keefler agreed to relieve Cabeldu of responsibility for the crossing, but ordered him to seize the enemy positions at the Beveland end of the Walcheren causeway. The Royals accomplished this task in a finely controlled night action which pinched off all the defenders by moving along the water's edge. They captured 153 prisoners and a great deal of equipment.

At 0930 hours on the morning of 31 October, Simonds decided to go ahead with the amphibious attacks on Walcheren Island and informed the Acting Corps Commander of this decision. Foulkes immediately sent a signal to 2nd Division headquarters which read, "No interference on Walcheren by guns or air. Most desirable we get on with it." The hazardous amphibious attacks on Flushing and Westkapelle were scheduled for dawn on 1 November and it was important to persuade the enemy that the attack would come from the Beveland area. The Scottish brigade had been scheduled to perform this task but it was so slow in arriving that Foulkes ordered Brigadier Megill to begin the operation by seizing a bridgehead on Walcheren which could then be turned over to the Scots.

The plan called for the Calgaries, who still had officers and NCOs trained for amphibious assaults, to cross the water obstacle in storm boats and tracked landing vehicles. The Maisonneuves would then be ferried over to join them. This action, coming hours before the seaborne invasion, would prevent the enemy from shifting troops to Flushing or Westkapelle and might result in the rapid occupation of Middelburg.

The Calgaries gained control of a bridgehead on Walcheren but the shelling intensified and "B" Company, hit by a heavy counterattack, was forced to retreat all the way to the edge of the causeway. "A" Company's only officer, Captain Wynn Lasher, was wounded and the situation seemed to be deteriorating. Major George Hees volunteered to take Lasher's place and the spare artillery FOO, Captain Walter Newman, asked to go along as second-in-command. While Newman had a well-deserved reputation for risk taking, Hees was a staff officer without combat experience, and so his offer was quite extraordinary. The Calgary CO, Lieutenant-Colonel Ross Ellis, on his way back to the island to obtain first-hand information, took the two men across and settled them in. The situation had deteriorated further and it was

The Walcheren causeway 4 November 1944. The Canadians were attacking east to west (right to left) against well-prepared German defences. The barren nature of the causeway is evident from this photo, with only shell craters and shattered trees to offer protection (the shadows of the trees are visible across the causeway). The two large craters (to the left of centre) were blown by German engineers to deny the causeway to vehicles.
LCMSDS Air Photo 235/3077

clear that the enemy was determined to prevent a breakthrough to Middelburg. At divisional headquarters Keefler was under considerable pressure from Foulkes. At 1630 hours Corps sent a signal which reported the interception of a German wireless message announcing that all German troops on Walcheren were "ready to surrender." The Corps Commander ordered his men "to push on and establish our bridgehead as soon as possible."

The landings at Flushing and Westkapelle were going well after some initial problems, and 5th Brigade was told to be prepared to hand over to 157th (Lowland) Infantry Brigade at 0600 hours the next morning. "It was stipulated however that a further attack would be necessary and the end of the Walcheren causeway firmly controlled before the relief took place."

The lead Maisonneuve company was in position at 0400 hours. Unfortunately the barrage, fired by 52nd Division artillery, began 300 yards short, striking the Calgary positions and delaying the Maisonneuves who were still 300 yards from the end of the causeway when the guns stopped. Megill ordered the Maisonneuves to dig in where they were and wait to be relieved by the Glasgow Highlanders but one company did not receive the order. They had made contact with the Calgary Highlanders and moved forward onto the island.

The Maisonneuve force consisted of about 40 men, including six volunteers from the Belgian White Brigade who had been with the battalion since September. Lieutenant Charles Forbes, heading 18 platoon, and Lieutenant Guy de Merlis, commanding 16 platoon, were skilled and aggressive leaders and the Maisonneuves worked their way forward to a position some 500 yards inland. A farmhouse became company headquarters, with the two platoons deployed back-to-back along the main road on both sides of the railway underpass. They were, however, totally isolated because the Calgaries had been withdrawn and "B" Company of the Maisonneuves was well back along the causeway.

Brigadier J.D. Russell, commanding 157th Brigade, had arrived on the night of 31 October. Russell was understandably unhappy at the prospect of sending one of his battalions into this chaotic battle. The divisional commander, Major-General E. Hakewill-Smith, had urged him to find an alternate way onto the island and

Destroyed Canadian tanks sit on the road to Wouwsche Plantage.
LCMSDS Photo

his engineers were searching for a route well to the south of the causeway. This sensible plan has been somewhat misrepresented in postwar accounts. The 52nd Division was planning to mount a carefully organized two-brigade attack as part of the overall battle for Walcheren Island. This action was expected to take some time and it is not difficult to understand why Hakewill-Smith challenged Foulkes when he was ordered to attack across the causeway. This dispute involved an issue quite separate from the decision to commit 5th Brigade on 31 October.

Russell agreed to take over the causeway bridgehead, but only with a minimum of troops. The Glasgow Highlanders sent two platoons forward, but they were forced to stop at the western edge of the causeway. At noon on 2 November the Maisonneuves were ordered to withdraw from the island. The Glasgow Highlanders dug in at the end of the causeway and held the position until the Scottish divisional engineers found a crossing near Nieuwdorp. By dusk on 3 November they had outflanked the enemy.

Fifth Brigade was by then on its way to Belgium for a long overdue rest. The causeway had cost the Calgaries 17 killed and 46 wounded. The Maisonneuves, with their companies of less than 60 men, had just one fatality and 10 men wounded. The battle for the causeway was not the ill-conceived disaster that it is so often portrayed. The Acting Corps Commander's order to mount an attack and maintain pressure was a necessary part of the overall plan to capture Walcheren Island. The operation itself was carried out with considerable skill and relatively small losses. On 20 October Field Marshal Montgomery, who had belatedly recognized the importance of the Scheldt, wrote a letter to Guy Simonds which was as close to an apology as Montgomery could offer: "I think everything you are doing is excellent, and your troops are doing wonders under the most appalling conditions of ground and weather. I doubt if any other troops would do it so well and I am very glad the Canadians are on the business. Please tell your chaps how pleased I am with their good work."

Bergen-op-Zoom

While 2nd Division fought its way to Walcheren, 4th Division employed two balanced brigade groups each with two infantry and two armoured battalions. This method, first developed in the late stages of the Normandy campaign, proved very effective in the first stages of Operation "Suitcase." The divisional plan called for Brigadier Robert Moncel's force to move in a wide circling movement to the north of Bergen-op-Zoom before Jefferson's brigade moved directly towards the city. Unfortunately, the advance to Wouwsche Plantage was contested by German armour that lay in wait guarding the narrow tracks that ran through extensive pine forests. Within minutes, enemy self-propelled

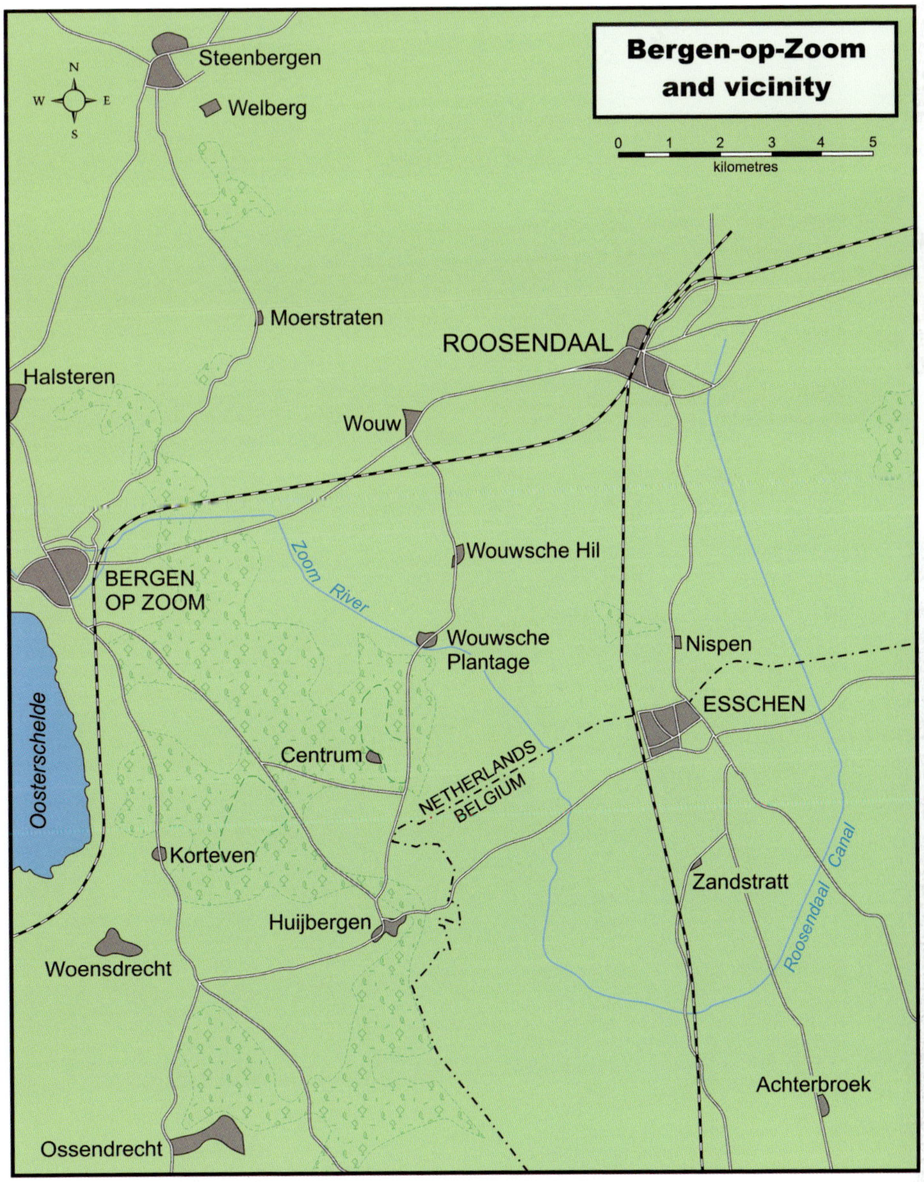

Right: Dutch children wave to passing Canadian tank crews in Bergen-op-Zoom, 29 October 1944.
LAC PA 131256

Below: Aerial Photograph of Bergen-op-Zoom taken 12 September 1944.
LCMSDS Air Photo Collection 166/3042

guns knocked out ten of the Grenadier Guards' tanks. When the Lake Superior Regiment moved to deal with the obstacle, the enemy withdrew to a reserve position. Infantry attacks, even with tank and artillery support, were complicated by the enemy's liberal use of minefields, including ones that had been booby-trapped to counter the pioneer platoons normal methods of defusing them. It took Moncel's force three days of bitter, costly fighting to reach the railway line northeast of Bergen-op-Zoom and by then Jefferson's brigade was on the outskirts of the town.

Signs of an enemy withdrawal were evident even after the capture of Wouwsche Plantage and a battlegroup of Lincs and South Albertas moved cautiously forward. Despite the darkness of the

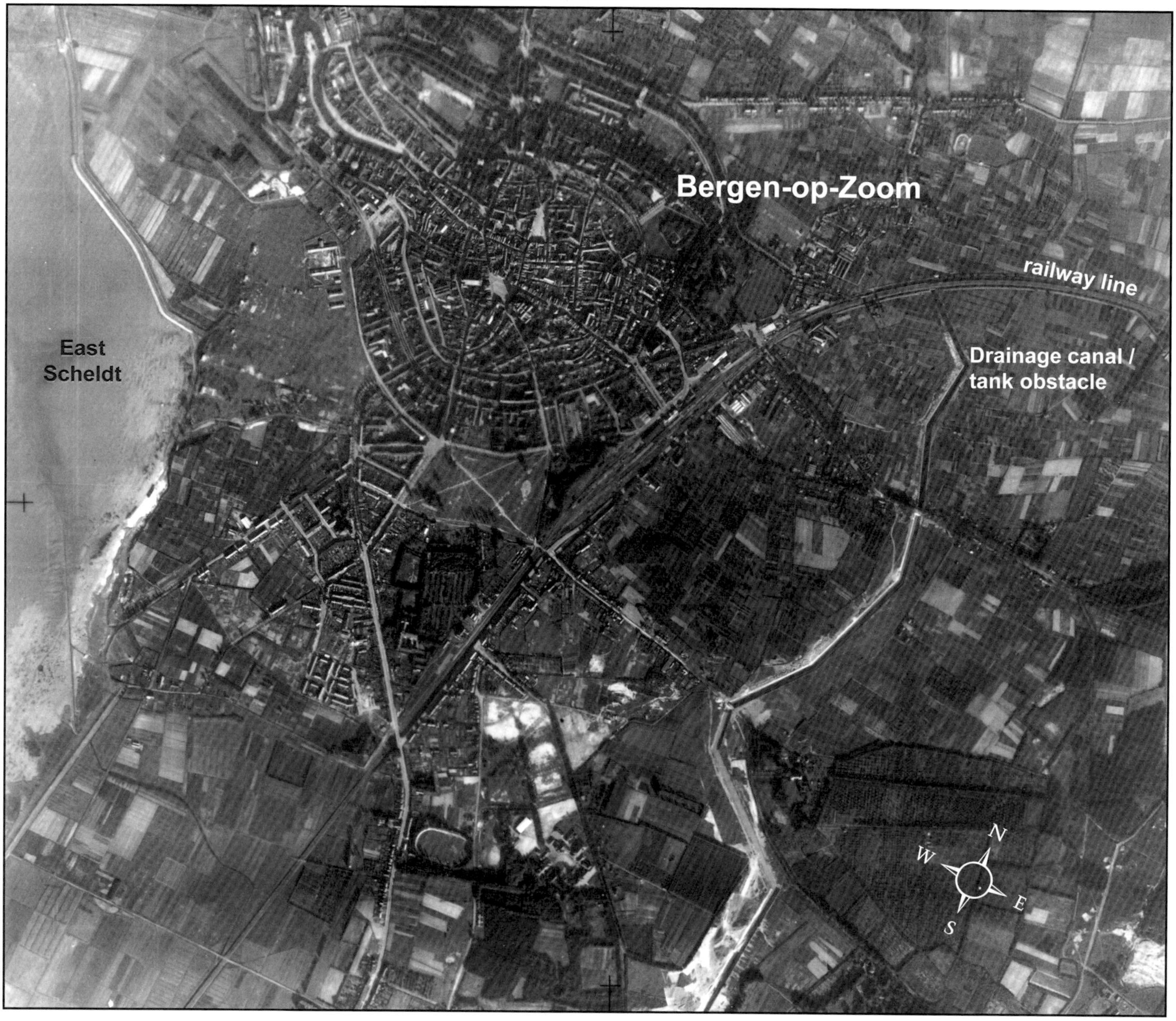

A young Dutch woman commands the full attention of troopers from the South Alberta Regiment, Bergen-op-Zoom, 29 October 1944.
LAC PA 140429

late afternoon, civilian reports that the enemy had withdrawn to a position on the northern edge of Bergen-op-Zoom tempted the two commanding officers if for no other reason than to get their men out of the pouring rain.

"Swotty" Wotherspoon of the South Albertas turned to Lieutenant-Colonel Bill Cromb and said: "Hell Bill, lets take the damn place." Major Jim Swayze, who commanded a Lincs company, got his men moving by telling them: "They're in there and they're nice and dry…Are we going to stay here and get soaked? No way." Swayze's men, with a squadron of tanks, advanced to the Grote Markt where the Hotel de Draak was commandeered. Tanks were soon stationed at the head of the northern facing streets with orders to keep the roads empty. The next morning, the Dutch flag flew proudly from the town hall for the first time since 1940.

But the battle for Bergen-op-Zoom was far from over. The situation along the Zoom River, where blown bridges and a line of anti-tank obstacles assisted the German defenders, remained precarious until the morning of 24 October. For the Argylls, Bergen-op-Zoom was anything but a happy adventure. The battalion was ordered to make a set-piece attack across the Zoom and the wide drainage canal that served as a tank obstacle. Short rounds from the medium artillery and well organized German resistance brought the first attempt to a grinding halt. Casualties from friendly fire were a constant problem in the Second World War, but since no one wanted to attack without the largest possible amount of support, accidental losses had to be accepted. A second attack also failed and this left a small group of Lincs, who had tried to divert German attention, isolated on the enemy side of the canal. Between 0300 hours and dawn, a third attempt brought some success and the Argylls and a company of Lincs began the difficult task of clearing close-packed buildings defended by enemy machine-guns. By mid-afternoon Jefferson committed the Algonquins and the South Albertas and both units helped complete the task. The Argylls had nine killed, 29 wounded. The Lincs had 11 killed, 27 wounded.

The German high command, with Hitler watching closely, decided to hold some bridgeheads south of the Maas River, a policy that was to cost their army and the Allies many casualties. When operations ended on 8 November, the Germans held just one bridgehead at Kapelsche Veer.

The enemy's decision to contest the Canadian advance became evident when Brigadier Moncel outlined plans for a rapid strike to Steenbergen, northeast of Bergen-op-Zoom. The Canadian Grenadier Guards were teamed with the Algonquin Regiment for a night advance that was supposed to reach the edge of Steenbergen while two infantry companies dealt with opposition from the nearby villages of Bocht and Welberg. Their cross-country attack on the villages quickly turned into a nightmare when both companies were overrun by German battlegroups led by self-propelled guns.

In this flat country, a slight rise, like the one at Welberg, dominated the area, and with many of the fields flooded and the roads mined, the armoured regiments could only provide indirect support. This meant a full-scale infantry attack with divisional artillery fire plan, medium artillery and all the Typhoon aircraft 84 Group could spare. The Algonquins and the Lincs launched the second attack on Welberg on 2 November. The artillery and a squadron of rocket-firing Typhoons turned the village into a blazing beacon giving the infantry enough light to advance.

Once in amongst the ruins, an intense close-quarters struggle lasted well past dawn. By then engineers had cleared the road and the self-propelled 17-pounders of the 5th Anti-Tank Regiment had moved up to deal with their enemy counterparts. The battles fought by 4th Canadian Armoured Division in October and November 1944 have been overshadowed by the more dramatic encounters at the Leopold Canal, Woensdrecht and the Walcheren causeway, but they were no less important and demanded no less courage or sacrifice.

Canadian armour and other vehicles in the main square of Bergen-op-Zoom, 31 October 1944.
LAC PA 142088

Memorial to the Essex Scottish Regiment in Putte.
Photos by J.A. Robertson

The Tour

For authenticity, you should begin the tour in Antwerp and along the Albert Canal. Antwerp is an interesting city to visit, but so much has changed since the war that it is almost impossible to visualize the areas that 4th Brigade fought over in 1944. Denis and Shelagh Whitaker, who visited Antwerp on several occasions since Brigadier Whitaker led the RHLI in the dock area, offered the following suggestions to those who wish to combine a battlefield tour with a visit to the city.

The port of Antwerp may be viewed by boat or by car. The boats leave from Quay 14 Londenbrug. There is also an evening dinner cruise. By car, you can follow the signs "Havenroute" but you will see much less of the dock areas. The municipal cemetery "Schoonselhof" includes the graves of 348 Canadian soldiers and airmen in a separate area. In the former village of Oorderen within the Port of Antwerp, there is a plaque at the General Motors Plant where the RHLI had their headquarters. There is a very impressive memorial to the Canadians and their partners in the Belgian resistance at Kalmthout and a plaque commemorating the RHLI on the riverfront.

There is a striking monument to the Essex Scottish Regiment in Putte. The inscription reads:

Across the frontiers of countries
Across the frontier of fear
Across the frontier of occupation
Across the frontier of life
Led their path to our freedom

You may prefer to bypass the Antwerp area and make a side trip to Putte and Kalmthout from Woensdrecht. On our tours we cross the Westerschelde (West Scheldt) and drive

Above: Air photo of Westkapelle showing the breach created in the dyke by RAF bombing. The damage caused by the bombing and flooding is clearly evident when compared with the "before" photo (inset). The lighthouse in Westkapelle, still prominent today, can be seen at the top of the photo (look for its shadow).
LCMSDS Air Photo 231/3029 & CFJIC PMR 83-759

Right: A British Flail (mine-clearing) Sherman tank comes ashore at Westkapelle.

to Westkapelle. The ferry between Breskens and Flushing (Vlissingen) no longer carries automobiles so you must use the new tunnel and follow the signs to Middelburg then Zoutelande and Westkapelle.

The assault on Westkapelle was one of the most difficult amphibious operations of the war and while the assault troops were British, the battle was planned and directed by Lieutenant-General Guy Simonds and his chief gunner (CCRA) Brigadier Bruce Matthews. The plan called for 4th Special Service Brigade to land in the gap created by bombing the Westkapelle dyke. The weather prevented air support and the bombing had not silenced the big gun batteries which controlled the approaches to the Port of Antwerp. The assault was supported by the guns of the battleship HMS *Warspite* and the monitor HMS *Roberts*

Right and Below: Sherman tank memorial to No.4 Commando Brigade (Royal Marines).

but it was the bravery of the naval personnel of the improvised "Support Squadron, Eastern Flank" that saved the Commandos from disaster. These modified landing craft, mounting 4.7-inch and 17-pounder guns provided such effective direct support that enemy fire was directed at them instead of the Commandos. As the flotilla commander noted "so long as the Germans made the mistake of concentrating their fire at the Support Squadron, close action was justified and losses acceptable…" Twenty of the 27 craft were sunk or damaged in the action but the Commandos were able

Right: Westkapelle today. The area of the breach (sandy beach at left of photo) is still clearly visible as a rough indentation along an otherwise smooth coastline. The small lake was created when the breach was sealed after the war.
Photo by Evert Stieber

Since the end of the Second World War the Dutch have been busy reclaiming land from the sea. As a result, Walcheren is no longer an island joined to the Beveland penisula by a narrow causeway. The original causeway still carries the main road and rail line to Walcheren and is marked by the row of trees crossing the middle of the photo from left to right. A small memorial park at the western end on the south side contains memorials to 5th Canadian Infantry Brigade (inset) as well as the 52nd (Lowland) Division and French army which fought in the region in 1940.
Air photo by Evert Stieber

to attain their objectives. The memorial on the dyke at Westkapelle uses a rebuilt Sherman Tank as the focal point. The tank faces the breach caused by the RAF bombing. From this vantage point, you can visualize much of the battle of November 1944.

Return to the A58 autoroute (Goes, Bergen-op-Zoom). Take Exit 37 at Arnemuiden and follow the road (N665) on the south side of the autoroute towards Lewedorp. The memorial to battalions of the 5th Canadian Infantry Brigade that attacked across the Walcheren Causeway is on the south side of the road at what was the western end of the causeway. The museum in Nieuwdorp, formerly named "Infatuate," is now a broader-based museum about the war in Beveland and is the centre for new initiatives including a liberation march scheduled for late October of each year. To reach Nieuwdorp continue on the service road crossing over the A58, turn right. You will find the village and museum well signed..

The causeway or Sloedam, as the Dutch call it, has long since disappeared. The railway line which runs alongside the autoroute marks the northern side of the embankment. Rejoin the autoroute at the next interchange to the east. Take the A58 autoroute east towards Hoogerheide, exit 30. Do not take the A4 South to Antwerp! On one of our battlefield tours I made this error, much to everyone's amusement. The N11 south will take you to Putte and Kalmthout. Return north on the N11 to Ossendrecht which the 4th Brigade

A small park in Woensdrecht honours the Fort Garry Horse (top) and the Royal Hamilton Light Infantry (above). A plaque honouring the Black Watch role in the battle was recently added.

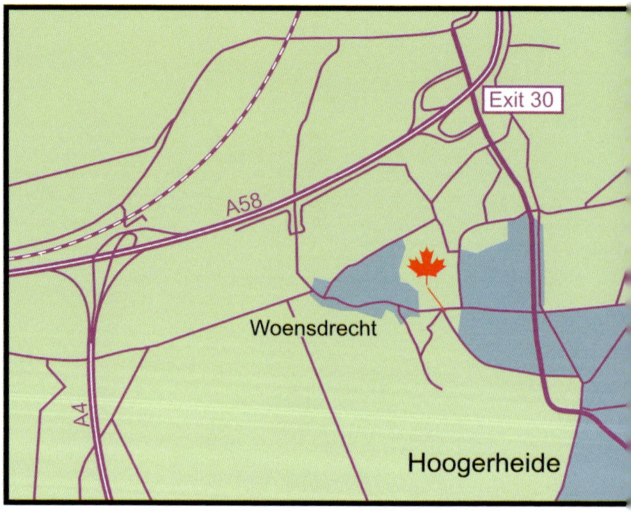

reached on the night of 6 October. Hoogerheide, Woensdrecht and Korteven were supposed to fall the next day but instead more than two weeks of intense combat was required.

To understand the struggle for the Woensdrecht area, it is best to see the battlefield from both the Canadian and the German perspective. Turn off the N11 to Woensdrecht pausing to visit the RHLI and Black Watch memorial in the village. The Royal Regiment reached the railway embankment at Volekerdorp to the west. The Black Watch attack of 13 October came from the west side of Woensdrecht directly across empty fields (which the A58 now occupies) to the railway. Van der Heydte's paratroopers were dug-in to the north side of the railway embankment. Artillery and mortar crews on the reverse slope of the Woensdrecht ridge to the east had good observation of all movement. It is difficult to imagine how any troops could have taken the position.

When the RHLI attacked and captured Woensdrecht, they challenged the paratroopers' hold on the area and were subjected to repeated counterattacks which caused heavy casualties to both sides. The Essex Scottish and an additional squadron of Fort Garry tanks were used to hold the ridge east of the village which the Rileys had seized on 16 October. The South Sasks destroyed the last enemy in the area a week later. The defensive battles fought by the South Sasks and

Maisonneuves in the Hoogerheide-Huijbergen area made a significant contribution to weakening the aggressive 6th Parachute Regiment. There is a liberation memorial in Huijbergen and an interesting war museum in Ossendrecht.

If you wish to explore 4th Division's "Green Route" north take the road from Huijbergen to Wouwsche Plantage. Fourth Armoured Division captured Wouwsche Plantage after a bloody encounter with a German armoured battlegroup which included a number of self-propelled 88 mm guns. It took three days of "nightmarish fighting" to force an enemy withdrawal. From Wouwsche Plantage continue north turning left towards Heerle. Cross the A58 and turn left on the service road to the Commonwealth War Cemeteries. The British cemetery is just east of the Bergen-op-Zoom Canadian War Cemetery. The Canadians here are largely from 2nd and 4th Divisions. It is the counterpart of the Adegem Cemetery for 3rd Division and taken together, they spell out the sacrifice Canadians made to open the port of Antwerp.

To visit Bergen-op-Zoom, continue east on the service road and follow signs to the Centrum. In 1944, the "Grote Markt" was full of South Alberta Regiment tanks and the Hotel de Draak was regimental headquarters for both the SARs and the Lincs. By accident, we met Major David Currie, VC and his wife in the restaurant here on our first tour of the battlefields. Major Currie told

Above: Soldiers from the 6th Field Park Squadron, Royal Canadian Engineers, repair the town sign for Bergen-op-Zoom, 29 October 1944.
LAC PA 113667

Right: Tanks and vehicles of the South Alberta Regiment in the Grote Markt in Bergen-op-Zomm, 28 October 1944.
LAC PA 131261

Soldiers of the Lincoln and Welland Regiment training for the attack on Kaplesche Veer, January 1945. LAC PA 142421

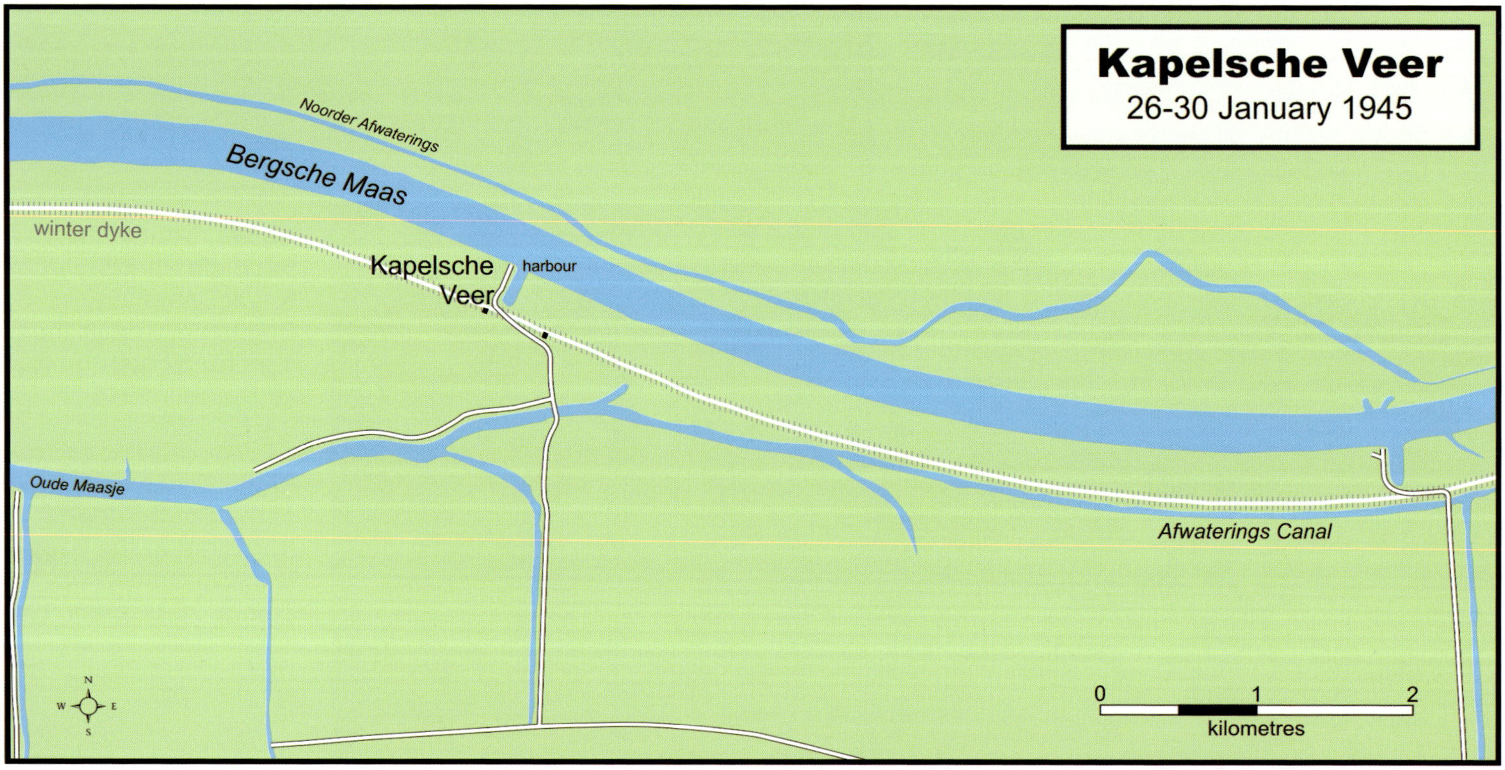

us that the Hotel used to feature photographs of the liberation but they are long gone. The only sign of October 1944 are plaques commemorating the South Alberta Regiment, the Argyll and Sutherland Highlanders and the Lincoln and Welland Regiment which may be found inside the 17th century Stadhuis (town hall). The bridge over the Zoom River has a small plaque noting the battle.

Once across the Zoom, 10th Brigade moved quickly north to Steenbergen while 4th Armoured Brigade cleared the coastal area. On 5 November, the motorized Lake Superior Regiment, with tanks of the British Columbia Regiment, reached

Kapelsche Veer as seen from the air today.

Top: The view looking southeast. The harbour and ferry crossing at Kapelsche Veer are in the centre and the small "L" shaped woods at the centre right mark the location of the memorial plaques.

Bottom: The view looking northeast. The harbour on the south bank is marked by the line of trees at the centre left of the photo. The canoe-borne assault by the Lincoln and Welland Regiment put into the water at the bend in the river at the top of the photo.

Air photos by Evert Stieber

the sea and fought one of the army's few naval engagements of the war, sinking three small German naval vessels in the harbour of Zijpe on the eastern end of Schouwen Island. This route may be retraced today, though at present there are no markers. Take the N259 to Steenbergen. The most difficult battle was fought at Welberg. Follow the N257 north exiting at Sint Philipsland and continue west to the harbour at Sluis. Zijpe is directly across the narrow strait.

Tracing the pursuit to the Maas will not be a priority for most visitors until something is done to commemorate these actions but a visit to Kapelsche Veer should be on everyone's itinerary. The battlefield may be reached from Exit 36 on the A59 just west of Waalwifle and s'Hertogenbosch. Follow the signs north to Kapelsche Veer. The original justification for evicting the enemy from this spot was the threat of a major counterattack across the Maas co-ordinated with the Ardennes Offensive. By 26 January when Operation "Elephant" began the Germans had been defeated in the Bulge and there was no possibility of using Kapelsche Veer as a bridgehead for a major operation. Since both the Polish Armoured Division and 47th Royal Marine Commando had failed to dislodge the enemy when it might have mattered, the decision to employ one Canadian infantry battalion in the initial attack when it did not is hard to fathom.

To complicate matters, Major-General Chris Vokes, commanding 5th Armoured Division, came up with a complex, seemingly clever plan involving assaults from each flank with a simultaneous waterborne attack using canoes. The enemy was so well dug-in that all the manoeuvring had little impact. Kapelsche Veer was eventually captured but the SARs, Lincs and Argylls did it using well-tried fire and movement employing artillery support co-ordinated by FOOs of the 15th Field Regiment. There is a small commemorative marker at the site of the battle.

Canadian operations in the Scheldt Estuary were essential to allow ships to reach the port of Antwerp. The Danish ship *Thyra III* and the Norwegian coaster *Lysland* were the first two Allied transports to enter Antwerp harbour after minesweepers finished clearing the channel, 26 November 1944. LAC PA 138404

The Rhineland and the Rhine Crossing

The year of victory, 1945, did not begin well for the Allies. The German army's Ardennes' offensive had been halted, but no one yet knew whether the Panzer Armies had been decisively defeated. The enemy had achieved complete surprise and made dramatic gains in the early stages of the "Battle of the Bulge," proving that the German army was still a dangerous adversary. Then on New Year's Eve Hitler launched another offensive (Operation "Nordwind") aimed at the southern flank of the Allied line. "Nordwind" was intended to force General Patton to turn away from the Ardennes and reinforce 6th US Army Group, but Eisenhower insisted on maintaining pressure on "the bulge" even at the cost of a temporary withdrawal in the south.

On New Year's Day the Luftwaffe, without any warning from Ultra, struck at Allied ground targets, particularly airfields. In more than 1,000 sorties, 300 Allied aircraft were destroyed for the loss of 200 German planes. In time it would become apparent that these offensives were a last, desperate bid to regain the initiative in the west, but in January no one was certain that the enemy had sacrificed resources vital to the defence of Germany.

The Allies were nervous and uncertain. The last available infantry division had been committed to battle and a serious reinforcement crisis loomed. The Canadians had been forced to bring 16,000 conscripts to Europe to meet their manpower needs and the British called up 250,000 additional men for their army. It is important to remember that no one knew when the war would end. On 12 January the British Cabinet suggested that the war in Europe might last until the end of 1945!

Allied plans for 1945 called for the elimination of enemy forces on the west bank of the Rhine as a prelude to the major operation against Germany. Plans for the

Transport aircraft towing gliders pass overhead during Operation "Varsity," the airborne crossing the Rhine, 24 March 1945.
CFJIC ZK 982-2

Two views of the aftermath of the New Year's attack by the Luftwaffe. Above: A fuel truck burns on the airfield at Eindhoven, Holland. Top right: The wreckage of a Spitfire sits in the foreground while the wing of a German aircraft shot down during the attack can be seen on the left.
LCMSDS Photo Collection

main assault across the Rhine had again pitted Montgomery against Eisenhower in a replay of the strategic debate which had raged since Normandy. Monty demanded priority for a northern offensive under his control, while Bradley and Patton pressed their case for parallel operations. Eisenhower assigned priority to the north, allotting 9th US Army and 1st Airborne Army to Montgomery, but 1st and 3rd US Armies were to advance to the Rhine and prepare their own operations to cross the river.

The first major offensives of the year were scheduled for early February. First Canadian Army, with Lieutenant-General Brian Horrock's 30th British Corps under command, was to carry out Operation "Veritable" as one arm of a pincer movement. The other arm was Lieutenant-General Bill Simpson's 9th US Army built up to a strength of ten divisions. Operation "Grenade" was supposed to begin two days after "Veritable," forcing the Germans to fight on two fronts. The weather and the enemy intervened. Flood waters from the Roer dams were released, turning the river into a raging torrent. "Grenade" was delayed for two weeks, but "Veritable" went ahead on 8 February.

Second Canadian Corps played a minor role in the first stage of "Veritable." Third Division, now nicknamed the "Water Rats," used Buffaloes, familiar from the Scheldt, to clear the flooded Rhine flank while 5th Brigade from 2nd Division captured the village of Wyler to open a supply route for 30th Corps.

Simonds was concerned about the slow pace and heavy casualties involved in the first phase of "Veritable" and he tried to persuade Montgomery to use 2nd Canadian Corps to jump the Rhine at Arnhem, instead of persisting with frontal attacks. Operation "Wallstreet" called for 49th

Bottom right: Warning sign posted upon entering Germany. Wyler, Germany, 10 February 1945.
LAC PA 145770

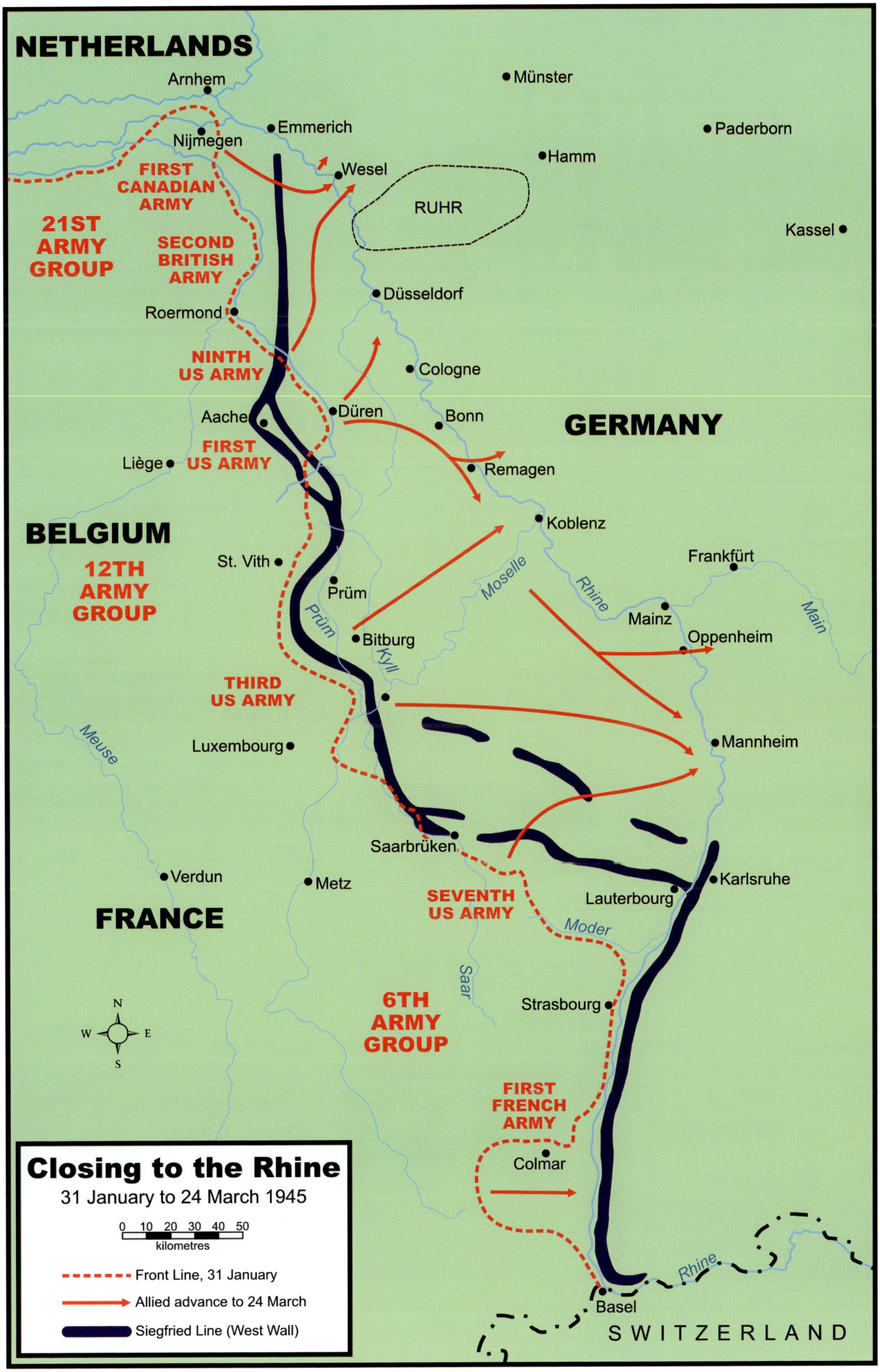
NETHERLANDS
Arnhem
Münster
Emmerich
Paderborn
Nijmegen
Hamm
Wesel
FIRST
CANADIAN
ARMY
RUHR
21ST
ARMY
GROUP
SECOND
BRITISH
ARMY
Kassel
Düsseldorf
Roermond
NINTH
US ARMY
Cologne
Aachen
Düren
Bonn
GERMANY
FIRST
US ARMY
Liège
Remagen
Koblenz
BELGIUM
12TH
ARMY
GROUP
St. Vith
Frankfürt
Prüm
Moselle
Rhine
Main
Mainz
Prüm
Bitburg
Oppenheim
Kyll
THIRD
US ARMY
Meuse
Luxembourg
Mannheim
Saarbrüken
Verdun
Metz
Karlsruhe
SEVENTH
US ARMY
Lauterbourg
FRANCE
Moder
Saar
6TH
ARMY
GROUP
Strasbourg
N
W
E
S
FIRST
FRENCH
ARMY
Colmar
Rhine
Basel
SWITZERLAND
Closing to the Rhine
31 January to 24 March 1945
0 10 20 30 40 50
kilometres
Front Line, 31 January
Allied advance to 24 March
Siegfried Line (West Wall)

Amphibious Buffaloes loaded with men from the North Shore (New Brunswick) Regiment head for the enemy. Near Nijmegen, Netherlands, 8 February 1945. LAC PA 140428

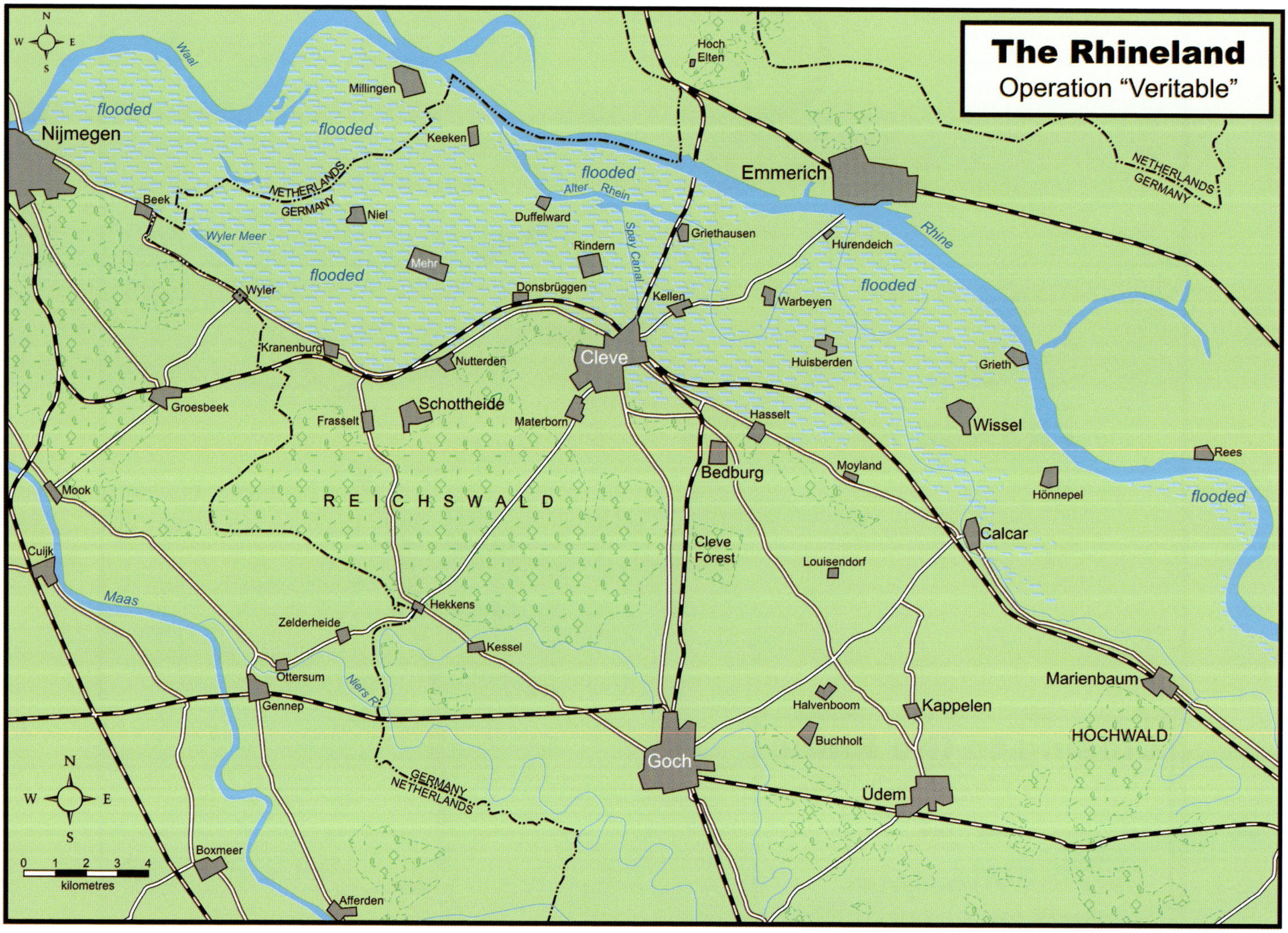

An aerial view of the heavily damaged town of Niel, Germany surrounded by water. This photo gives a good idea of the challenges faced by 3rd Canadian Infantry Division during the opening stages of Operation Veritable. Niel was captured by the Canadian Scottish Regiment (mounted in Buffaloes) on the morning of 9 February 1945.
LAC PA 145759

(West Riding) Division to lead the assault in Buffaloes "without preliminary bombardment." Simonds and Major-General G.H.A. Macmillan, the divisional commander, were confident Arnhem could be captured quickly. Corps engineers would then bridge the Rhine and the Canadian divisions would advance into the bridgehead. Simonds argued that the capture of Arnhem would force the Germans into headlong retreat. Montgomery was not interested. His purpose was to destroy German forces in the Rhineland and he intended to do this in a series of set-piece, attritional battles.

The Canadians re-entered combat on 15 February when 3rd Division took over the left flank from 15th Scottish Division. Their first task was to clear towards Louisendorf and occupy the wooded area near the village of Moyland. The Scots had suffered dreadful casualties at Moyland Wood in what they described as their "worst experience since the campaign began." Seventh Canadian Brigade, which took over the task, soon agreed. The enemy held the Moyland-Calcar sector in strength and were supported by artillery firing from the north bank of the Rhine.

The Royal Winnipeg Rifles secured Louisendorf but the Regina Rifles suffered more than 100 casualties trying to clear Moyland Wood. The enemy was able to reinforce the area and there

Troops of the 20th Field Company, Royal Canadian Engineers, handle a Bailey ferry service through the flooded area near Cleve, Germany, 23 February 1945
LAC PA 145759

Moyland Castle
LAC PA 183985

Two soldiers from Le Régiment de Maisonneuve guard the main entrance to Moyland Castle, 22 February 1945.
DND Army Photo 26825

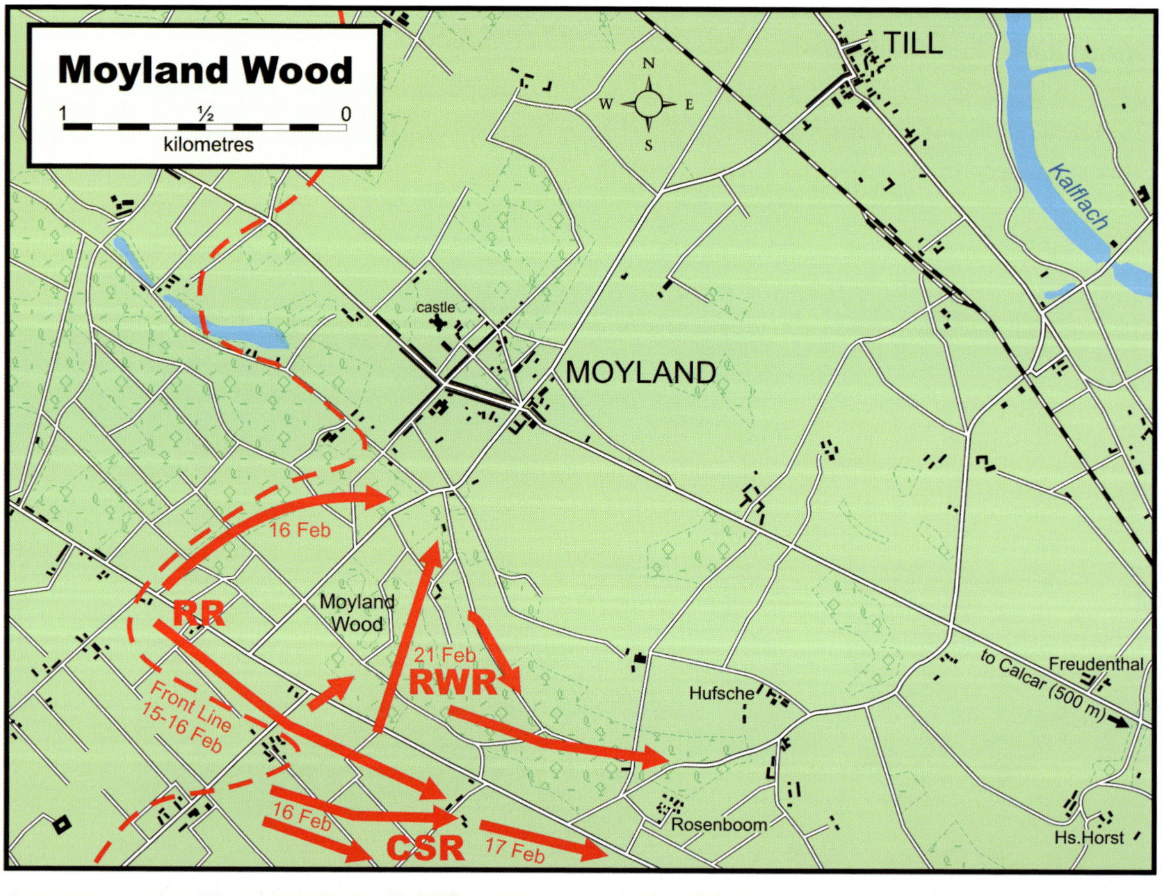

was no way one battalion could rout well dug-in paratroops with unlimited artillery support. The Canadian Scottish were also roughly handled and the intervention of the Fort Garry Horse could not prevent further heavy losses, including 53 men taken prisoner. General Simonds was unhappy with the way Major-General Dan Spry handled the battle, but for the moment it was Brigadier Jock Spragge who was replaced. Lieutenant-Colonel A.S. Gregory, the calm, tireless CO of the Reginas, took over the brigade and mounted a carefully co-ordinated attack using divisional mortars and artillery to blast the area sector by sector.

The Royal Winnipeg Rifles left their slit trenches near Louisendorf and moved into position south of Moyland Wood. Brigadier E.R. Suttie, who had replaced Brigadier Stanley Todd in command of the Divisional Artillery, prepared an elaborate fire plan involving medium and field artillery plus mortars, anti-tank guns, machine-guns and the tanks of the Fort Garry Horse. Gregory and Lieutenant-Colonel Lockie Fulton, the aggressive young commander of the Royal Winnipeg Rifles, devised a plan to clear the eastern end of the wood combining Wasps with tank support and air attacks. Each of the two lead companies kept three Wasps forward with three in reserve ready to leapfrog forward when fuel for the flame was exhausted. This continuous support boosted the morale of the assaulting troops while breaking the will of the enemy.

The Royal Winnipeg Rifles displayed outstanding skill as well as courage in the day-long battle that cost the battalion more than 100 casualties, 26 of them fatal. Major L.H. Denison, who led "D" Company in the final stages, received the Distinguished Service Order for his inspired leadership. Lieutenant George Aldous, temporarily blinded by grenade fragments, returned to his platoon after first aid treatment and led it in defeating repeated enemy counterattacks. He received the Military Cross.

Total casualties to the brigade, including battle exhaustion, exceeded 500 men and the westerners had to be pulled out of action. When it came time to sum up the lessons learned, emphasis was

Soldiers from the Regina Rifles prepare to attack Calcar, Germany, 16 February 1945.
LAC PA 177577

placed on the method of employing the flame-throwers, close contact between infantry and tanks and the 100 sorties flown by 84 Group of 2nd Tactical Air Force. No one mentioned the most important lesson – the enemy was fighting with a new intensity in defence of the Fatherland. German reports on the battle admitted great losses but insisted the decision to withdraw was made to straighten-out a "projecting front line" and "obtain reserves," the usual rationalization offered by German officers defeated in battle.

While the battle for Moyland raged, 2nd Division took over the Louisendorf sector and started an advance towards Calcar ridge. Fourth Brigade led off, reaching the Goch-Calcar road. Battlegroups from Panzer Lehr and 116th Panzer Divisions mounted immediate counterattacks and another bitterly fought struggle erupted. The Essex Scottish and Royal Hamilton Light Infantry dug-in and their FOOs called down defensive fire but with nightfall the Essex were overrun, as was "C" Company of the Rileys. Lieutenant-Colonel Whitaker of the RHLI organized his own counterattack and Brigadier Cabeldu sent the Royal Regiment and two companies of the Queen's Own Cameron Highlanders to restore the Essex position. The next day further attacks were beaten off at heavy cost to the enemy. Canadian losses were also high with the casualty toll reaching 400 men.

The battle for the Goch-Calcar road provides a good case study of both Allied and German battle doctrines in 1945. Second Division used a rolling barrage of 450 guns to get 4th Brigade on to its objectives. The assault companies were brought forward in "Kangaroo" armoured personnel carriers. The reserve companies moved up quickly to help form battalion fortresses. A limited objective was taken at relatively light cost. German doctrine called for immediate counterattacks and battlegroups composed of tanks or self-propelled guns supported by infantry rushed to overwhelm the defenders. As darkness fell, Canadian armour, rigidly following a doctrine practised throughout 21st Army Group, withdrew. Anti-tank defence now depended on battalion 6-pounders and the 2nd Anti-Tank Regiment RCA. Fortunately 18th Battery was equipped with 17-pounders which were highly effective against all German armour. This RCA battery alone destroyed seven German AFVs. The enemy's mobile reserves were used up in counterattacks which did not produce results. The

Canadian infantry in Cleve, Germany, 23 February 1945.
LCMSDS Photo

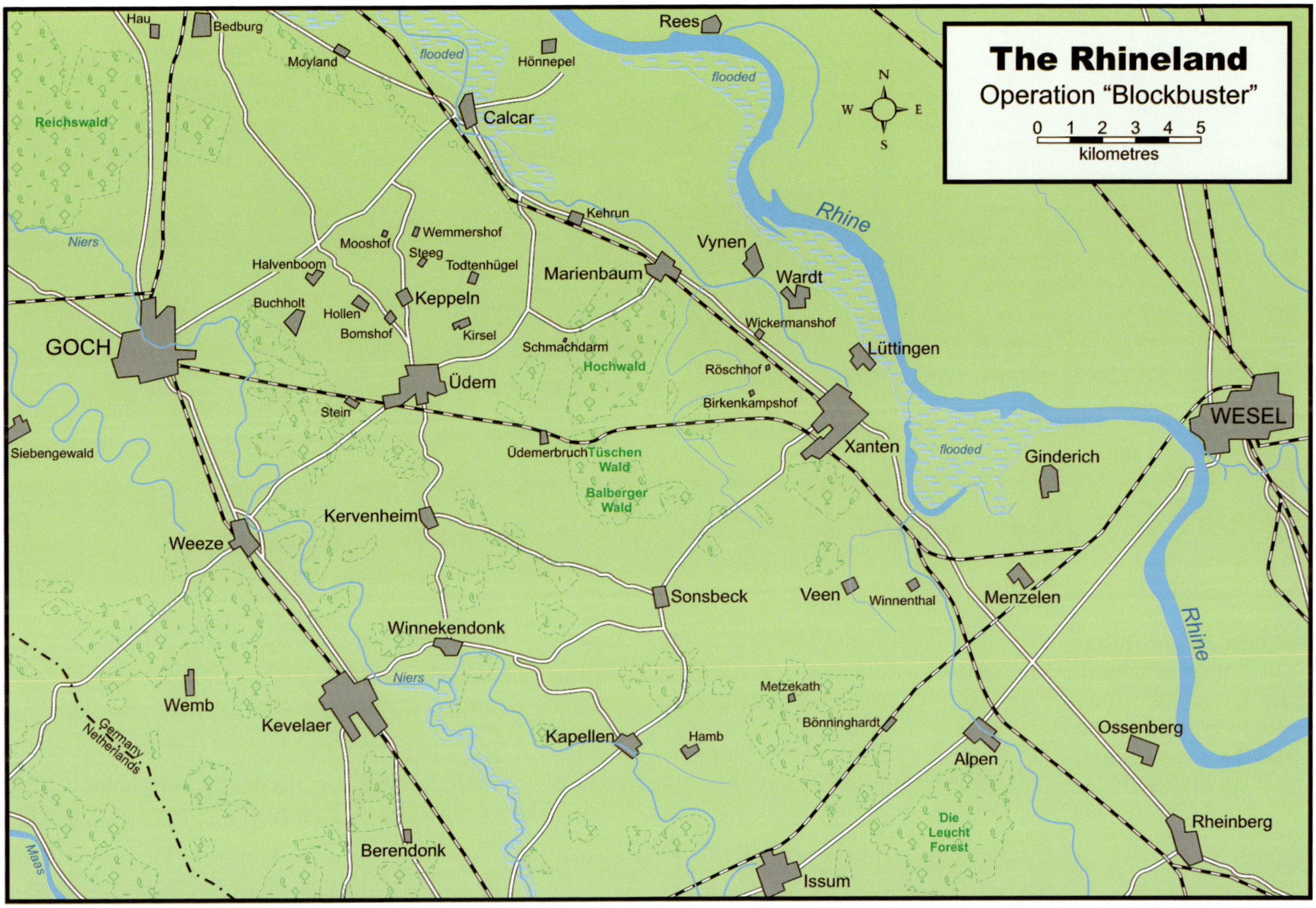

German doctrine "to strike the enemy before he can improve his position" may have been sensible when the Wehrmacht was winning, but in 1945 it was a disastrous policy.

"Veritable" came to an end on the 22 February and the next night the American army commander, General Bill Simpson, gambled on an assault crossing of the Roer before the flood waters had fully receded. The attack was made without a preliminary artillery barrage. Within 24 hours Ninth Army had 28 battalions across the river. There were only two German divisions left in the south and both were quickly destroyed. On the 25th Simpson reported that "there was not much in front of Ninth Army." Montgomery urged Simpson to strike for the Rhine and then turn north to Wesel trapping the enemy on the west bank. Rapid success would depend upon a renewal of the Canadian and British offensive to prevent the Germans from shifting resources to check the American advance. Panzer Lehr had already moved south and other units would soon join them if the pressure eased.

The Canadians launched Operation "Blockbuster" on 26 February in a series of well-executed attacks which secured the Calcar ridge. Sixth Brigade led off. The FMR, in the centre, leaned into the barrage and was quickly on its objective "taking a heavy toll of the enemy." The South Sasks, on the left, attacked the "pimple" at the peak of the ridge and with the support of Sherbrooke tanks crushed an enemy counterattack, and "all who survived were taken prisoner." The Camerons encountered soft ground and mines before finding an indirect route to their objective. Here a ferocious battle erupted as successive counterattacks were turned back. Fifth Brigade had been equally successful with the Black Watch, fully recovered from the effects of the Scheldt, especially effective.

In 3rd Division's sector the countryside was open and flat with each village and farmstead

A German Jagdpanther (self-propelled anti-tank gun) knocked out by Canadian troops in the Reichswald Forest, 15 March 1945.
LAC PA 137733

turned into a miniature fortress by the Germans. The artillery could suppress enemy fire during the advance but good infantry-tank co-operation was required to clear the strong points. Sergeant Aubrey Cosens of the Queen's Own Rifles received the Victoria Cross for his courage and skill at Mooshof and there were many other heroes that day. At Keppeln the North Shores encountered especially strong resistance which required a new set-piece attack. The delay jeopardized the advance of the Chaudières who described the fighting south of Keppeln as among the most difficult encountered in the war. Tanks of the First Hussars were crucial to the success of these small battles. Military historians who criticize the Allies for failing to develop good infantry-tank co-operation would do well to examine the role played by 2nd Canadian Armoured Brigade in the Rhineland.

Sergeant Aubrey Cosens of the Queen's Own Rifles was awarded a posthumous Victoria Cross for his outstanding actions at Mooshof, Germany which allowed the town to be captured in the face of fierce enemy resistance.
LAC PA 166764

Fourth Canadian Armoured Division entered the battle in the late afternoon. Brigadier Robert Moncel's "Tiger Force" (BCRs, CGGs, Lincs, Argylls) captured Todtenhügel. "Smith Force" (GGFG, Lake Superiors) took the next bound reaching Katzen-Berg despite darkness and scattered opposition. It had been a superb day for 4th Division and 9th Brigade was equally effective in the fight for Üdem. The 116th Panzer Division was forced to give up vital ground and 500 prisoners.

The same night, 4th Division's "Lion Group" (SARs, Algonquins) set out for Üdemerbruch and the high ground, Point 73, which dominates the western end of the "Hochwald Gap." Simonds, and 4th Division's GOC Major-General Chris Vokes, must have believed German resistance had been broken for they overruled the CO of the South Albertas who thought a night advance deep into enemy territory was unwise. At first all went well as one part of "Lion Group" reached the Goch-Xanten railway line but the Germans quickly concentrated all available resources

against this isolated spearhead. Brigadier Jefferson, commanding "Lion Group," was given control of his two other infantry battalions, the Lincs and Argylls, and thus began the bloody struggle for the Hochwald Gap.

To the senior commanders, these actions, lasting from 28 February to 3 March, may have been viewed as part of a co-ordinated offensive, but this was not apparent to anyone at the sharp end. The Allies had gradually perfected a battle doctrine which suited the equipment, training and morale of their citizen armies. Objectives could almost always be taken and held if the attack was built around a carefully prepared artillery program.

The purpose of such operations was to force the enemy to leave his prepared positions and counterattack. The German army in the west was destroyed in these set-piece battles but many Allied generals found this method too slow and too lacking in opportunities to demonstrate their skills as great commanders. Often they were persuaded, or persuaded themselves, that German resistance was weak and that adventurous offensive manoeuvres would work. Failure was

A Sherman tank (left) and a Stuart tank (right) of the South Alberta Regiment advancing into Veen, Germany, 7 March 1945.
LAC PA 113677

An oblique air photo of the German defences outside Üdem. Note the anti-tank ditch on the left and the smaller trenches to the right.
LAC PA 145740

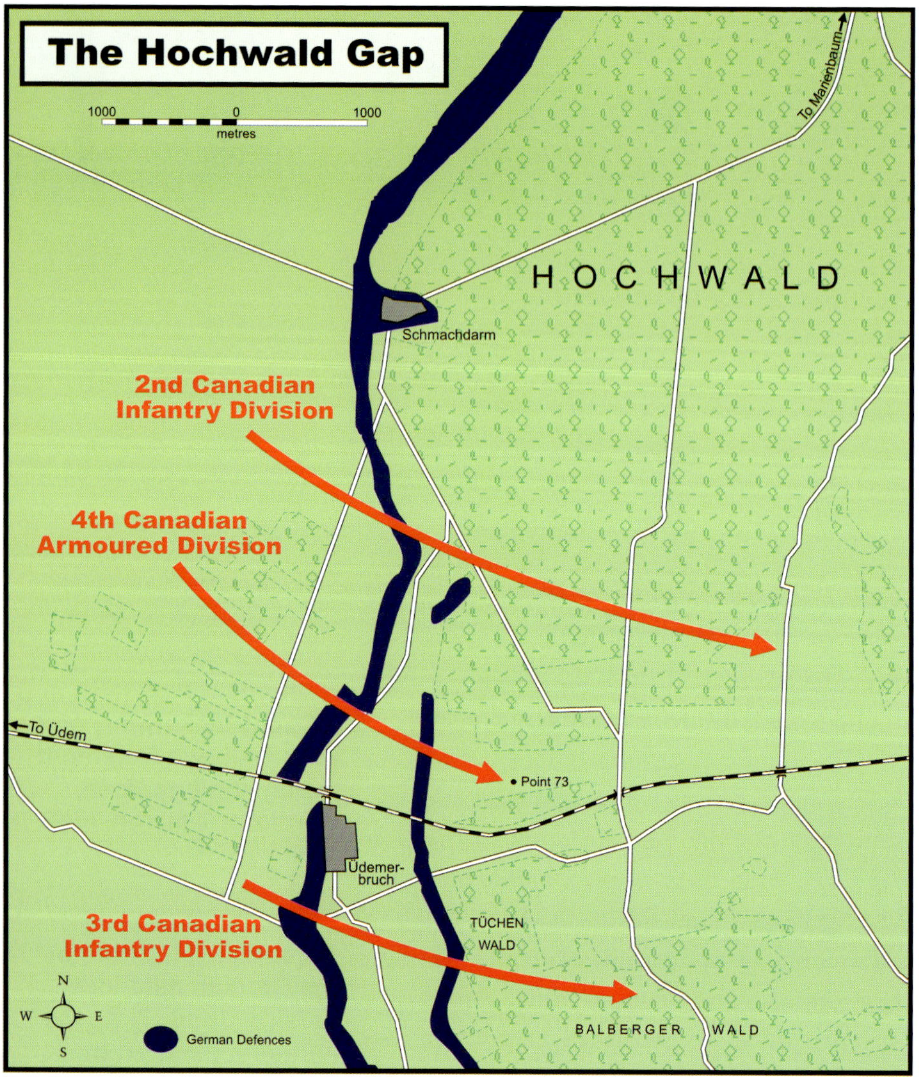

then attributed to "the lack of aggressiveness of the infantry" or "the caution of armoured units."

The reality is that no armoured unit, least of all a Sherman-equipped armoured brigade, could lead advances unless enemy anti-tank guns had been overcome. In the Hochwald Gap 4th Armoured Division was asked to attack an enemy which was being steadily reinforced and supported by numerous artillery and anti-tank gun batteries. The Argylls and Lincs were quickly pinned down by fire of "unbelievable intensity." Shortly before midnight the Grenadier Guards and British Columbia Regiment were sent forward. Fourth Armoured Brigade's war diary reported "the enemy guns took such a heavy toll, movement became impossible."

To the north 5th Brigade had begun a second advance into the Hochwald. The Calgaries broke through the "Schlieffen Line" but once in the forest the Brigade was struck by the same heavy artillery fire that had stopped "Lion Group." Simonds now committed everything he had. Fourth Brigade advanced into the northern part of the forest lead by the Essex Scottish. Major Fred Tilston was awarded his Victoria Cross for his actions in this battle. The RHLI took over from the Essex advancing along the road to Marienbaum.

South of the Gap the Chaudières led 8th Brigade into the Tüschen Wald while 4th Division and 6th Brigade made a new attempt to advance. On the morning of 2 March three Canadian and three British Divisions were inching forward, taking and inflicting heavy casualties. The impact of the American advance was first felt on the British front where 3rd British Division and the 6th Guards Tank Brigade had been fighting for every foot of ground. Suddenly they found the enemy gone. The Germans had withdrawn to a new and hastily improvised position called "the Wesel Pocket."

The Canadian role in the reduction of this last position west of the Rhine was centred on the capture of Xanten. Fourth Division fought its way into Veen while 2nd Division regrouped on the Calcar-Xanten road. Major-General Bruce Matthews was determined to control the Xanten battle and to this end he planned an all-arms operation built around an elaborate fire plan.

Major Fred Tilston of the Essex Scottish Regiment was awarded the Victoria Cross for outstanding gallantry while leading his company during an attack on 1 March 1945. Tilston was wounded three times during the battle and lost both his legs an a result of those injuries.
Canadian Forces Photo Unit ZK 1000

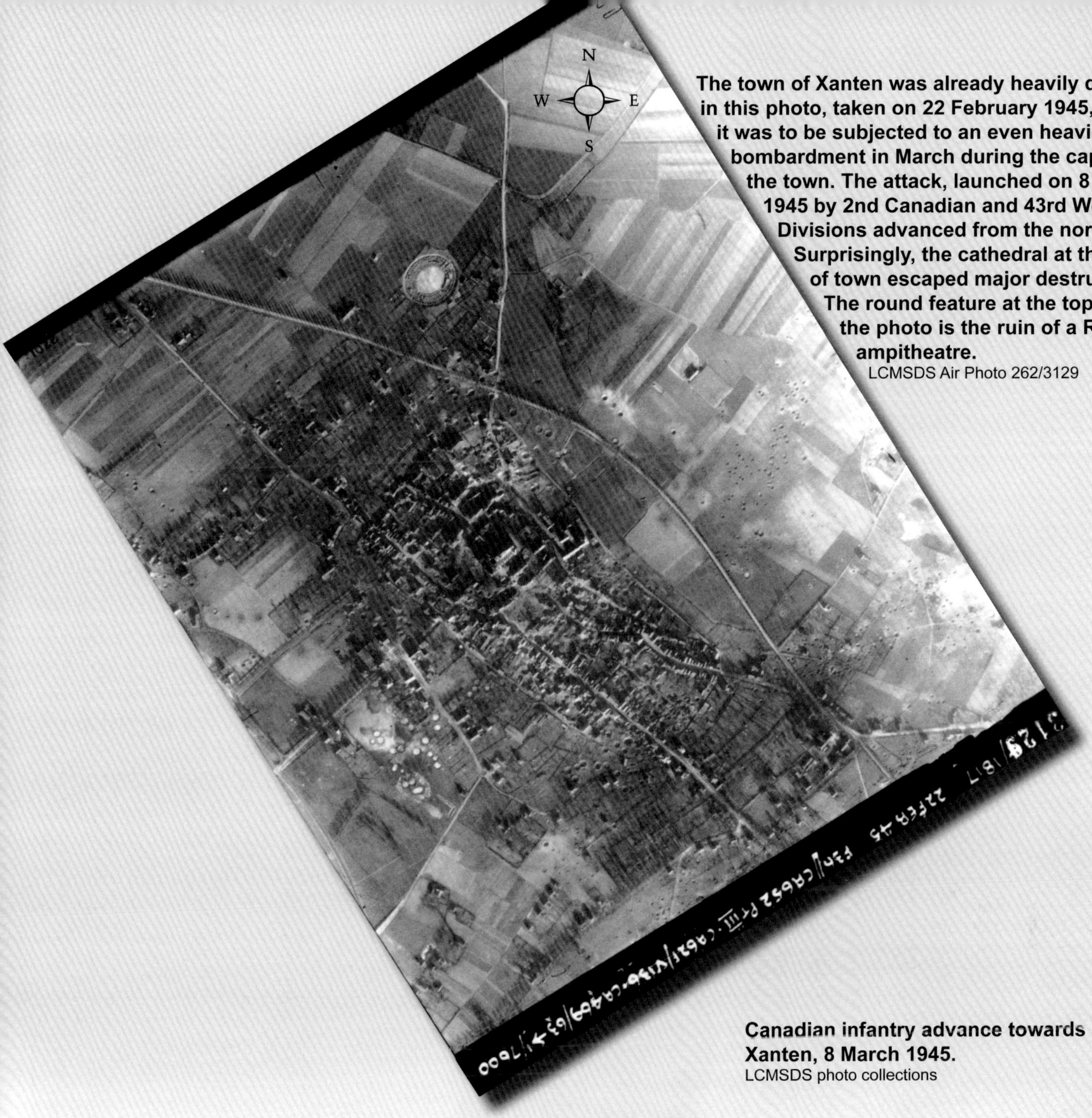

The town of Xanten was already heavily damaged in this photo, taken on 22 February 1945, but it was to be subjected to an even heavier bombardment in March during the capture of the town. The attack, launched on 8 March 1945 by 2nd Canadian and 43rd Wesex Divisions advanced from the northwest. Surprisingly, the cathedral at the centre of town escaped major destruction. The round feature at the top of the photo is the ruin of a Roman ampitheatre.
LCMSDS Air Photo 262/3129

Canadian infantry advance towards Xanten, 8 March 1945.
LCMSDS photo collections

Xanten, already heavily bombed, was blasted by corps and divisional artillery before 4th Brigade and 129th Brigade from 43rd British Division advanced on either side of the main road. Fifth Brigade delivered the final blow advancing to Birten before the retreating enemy blew the last bridge at Wesel.

Hitler had devoted enormous resources to the defence of the Rhineland because defeat would expose Germany's industrial heartland, the Ruhr, to direct attack. The month-long battle had resulted in a major Allied victory but at an enormous cost in human suffering.

A Canadian Sherman rumbles into the town of Xanten.
LCMSDS Photo Collection

* * * * *

The decisions to destroy the German army west of the Rhine and then cross the river in a major operation north of the Ruhr was made in December 1944 before the German Ardennes offensive. The Rhine crossing, code-named "Plunder," was to be the major Allied effort to end the war by striking in a "single thrust" for Berlin. At the Malta Conference in early February 1945, the Supreme Commander, General Eisenhower, revised this conception of the invasion of Germany with a plan which allowed for a second major Rhine crossing, south of the Ruhr.

On 7 March, while the battle of the Wesel pocket still raged, troops of the First US Army seized the Rhine bridge at Remagen and quickly established a substantial bridgehead on the east bank of the river. Since Montgomery did not plan to cross the Rhine until late March, the success of First US Army presented the Allied command with a major dilemma. Both the army commander, Courtney Hodges, and his superior, Omar Bradley, were reasonably confident that a breakout from the Remagen bridgehead could

A Canadian Sherman Firefly, mounting a 17-pounder gun, churns through the mud near Xanten, 9 March 1945..
LCMSDS Photo Collection

be staged whenever permission was granted. Eisenhower, perhaps fearing an even more serious row with the British, ignored intelligence estimates of German weaknesses and ordered Hodges to limit the bridgehead and use it as a device to draw the German reserves away from the north.

The bridgehead was certainly successful in this role, for by 23 March, the day of "Plunder," the Germans had moved most of their reserves opposite the Remagen bridgehead and had even attempted a counterattack. The next day, with the northern Rhine crossing safely launched, First US Army was unleashed. In a matter of a few hours it had brushed aside the German defenders and was racing forward into Germany with three armoured divisions in the lead. General Patton's

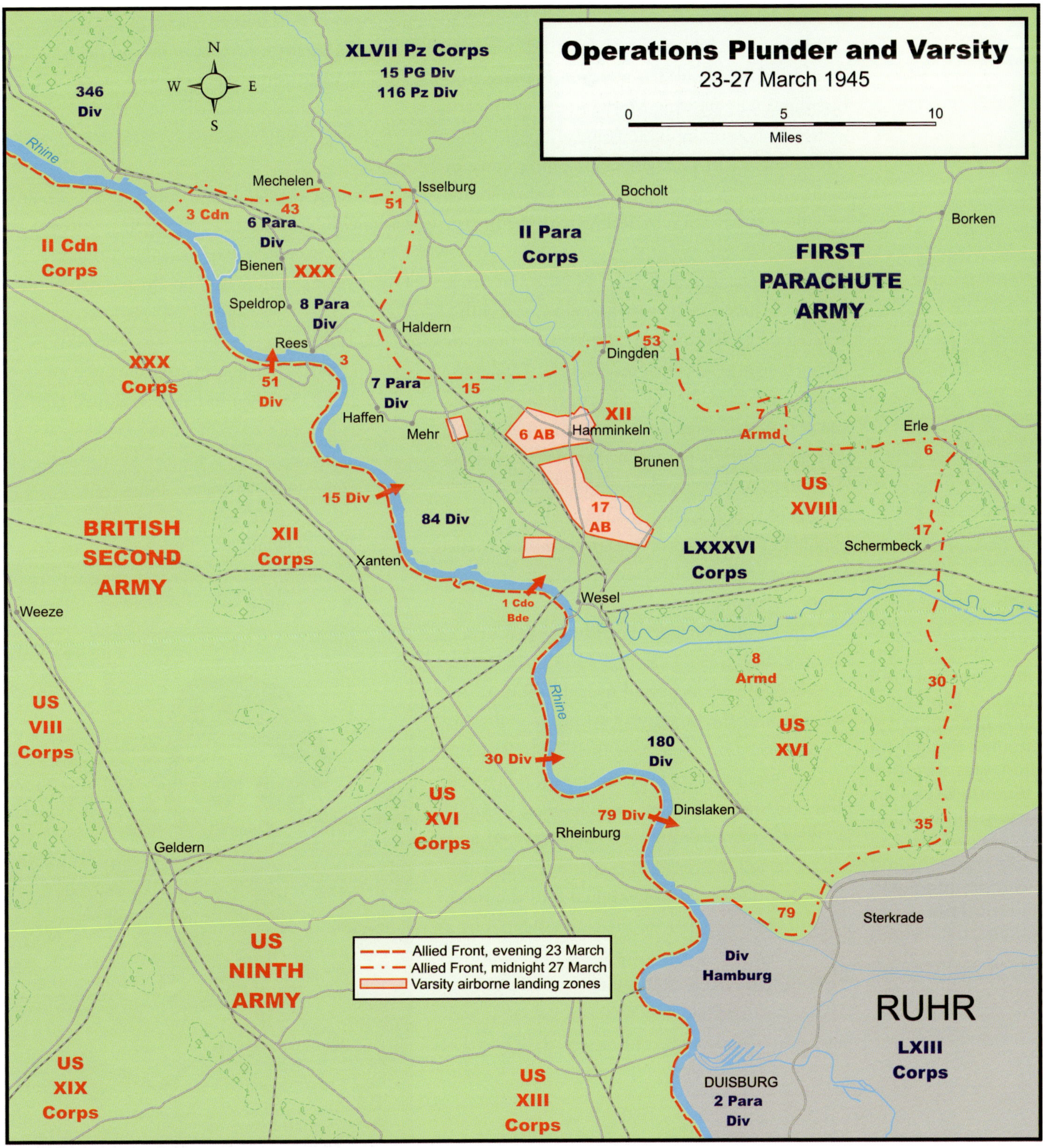

Third Army also crossed the Rhine before 24 March, but this was a deliberate demonstration of Patton's contempt for Montgomery's elaborate preparations. Patton announced that the Rhine could be crossed at any point without aid of preliminary artillery bombardment – nevermind with airborne divisions – and then released the news that they had done so "at a time calculated to take some of the lustre from news of Montgomery's crossing." All of this, no doubt, sounds somewhat childish, but the image of feuding generals should not be allowed to obscure the fact that Eisenhower, in allowing Montgomery to proceed with an elaborate amphibious and airborne battle, was paying a stiff price for maintaining unity in coalition warfare. It was a price that he would not be willing to pay again in dealing with the British commander.

The east bank of the Rhine opposite 21st Army Group was defended by two German Corps with a fighting strength of around 20,000 men. The 47th Panzer Corps, in reserve, possessed 35 to 40 tanks, and an equal number of self-propelled guns. To attack this pitiful remnant of the German Army with an airborne corps and two armies, supported by limitless air power and more than 2,500 artillery guns, could not fail to bring quick results. The 51st Highland Division was across in six minutes. The 1st Commando Brigade landed easily and cleared Wesel during the night.

Operation "Varsity," the airborne part of the crossing, began early on the 24th when a vast armada of aircraft appeared over the Rhine. The paratroops of the 6th British Airborne and 17th US Airborne Divisions made their drops without undue casualties, but by 1030 hours, when the gliders of the air landing brigades were coming in, the German flak gunners had recovered and a terrible toll was exacted. On the ground the airborne troops were soon engulfed in the most difficult and costly part of the entire operation.

The 6th British Airborne Division, including 1st Canadian Parachute Battalion, was dropped on the British front between Wesel and Rees. It was part of 3rd Parachute Brigade assigned to clear the Diersfordt Woods. During the course of the battle, which cost the battalion 43 casualties, a medical orderly, Corporal F.G. Topham, was awarded the Victoria Cross. The citation reads in part:

> Corporal Topham went forward through intense fire to replace the orderlies who had been killed before his eyes. As he worked on the wounded, he was himself shot through the nose. In spite of severe bleeding and intense pain, he never faltered in his task. Having completed immediate first aid he carried the wounded men steadily and slowly back through continuous fire...

One of the fatal casualties was Lieutenant-Colonel J. Nicklin, the commanding officer of 1st Canadian Parachute Battalion. His Brigadier, S.J. Hill, paid this tribute to Nicklin and his men:

> They really put up a tremendous performance [in "Varsity"] Unfortunately the price was high in that they lost their Colonel, Jeff Nicklin, who was one of the best fellows that I have met, and was the ideal man to command that Battalion...I only hope that the people back in Canada appreciate the really wonderful job of work he has done in producing his Battalion at the starting line in such outstanding form.

Right: Corporal Fred "Toppy" Topham, a medical orderly in 1st Canadian Parachute Battalion, was awarded the Victoria Cross for his actions in treating casualties, at great peril to himself, after parachuting into the Rhine bridgehead with his unit. This photo was taken on 8 August 1945.
Canadian Forces Photo Unit ZK 1032-3

Above: Transport aircraft towing gliders cross Allied lines on their way to the landing zones for Operation "Varsity," 24 March 1945.
Canadian Forces Photo Unit ZK 982-1

Right: Lieutenant-Colonel Fraser Eadie, commander of 1st Canadian Parachute Battalion, inspects his unit. Eadie took over the battalion after its former commander, Jeff Nicklin, was killed during "Varsity."
LAC PA 114745

These air photos show the airborne forces crossing the Rhine on their way to the landing zones (note each transport is towing two gliders) and on one of the "Varsity" landing zones, 24 March 1945.
LCMSDS Air Photo Collection

On the ground the 9th Canadian Infantry Brigade, attached to 51st Highland Division, crossed the Rhine early on the morning of the 24th. They took over the battle for Speldrop using heavy concentrations of medium artillery and Wasp flamethrowers. The balance of Brigadier Rockingham's brigade, plus the North Shore Regiment, was used to press forward northwest of Rees. Unfortunately, the 15th Panzer Grenadier Division had arrived to block the advance and when the North Novas attacked the village of Bienen they were badly mauled losing 114 men including 43 killed. The initial advance had been supported by "heavy artillery fire including a liberal use of smoke…" because the approach was over 300 yards of flat ground. The companies were brought under heavy fire before the barrage started and when the supporting fire began, the advance took place under conditions of growing confusion. That night, after a 3rd Anti-Tank Regiment battery of Self-Propelled Valentine 17-pounders had beaten off an armoured counterattack, the HLI advanced through the North Novas to complete the capture of the village.

The 7th Infantry Brigade had crossed into the bridgehead on the 27th and that night they staged a rapid attack on Emmerich. Major-General R.H. Keefler had replaced Spry in command of 3rd Division on 24 March, and this was his first battle as divisional commander. In three days of carefully controlled fighting for the city, the Brigade suffered 122 casualties including 44 killed. Emmerich had been reduced to rubble by bombs and shells, but the enemy used the rubble to defend the city with unbelievable determination.

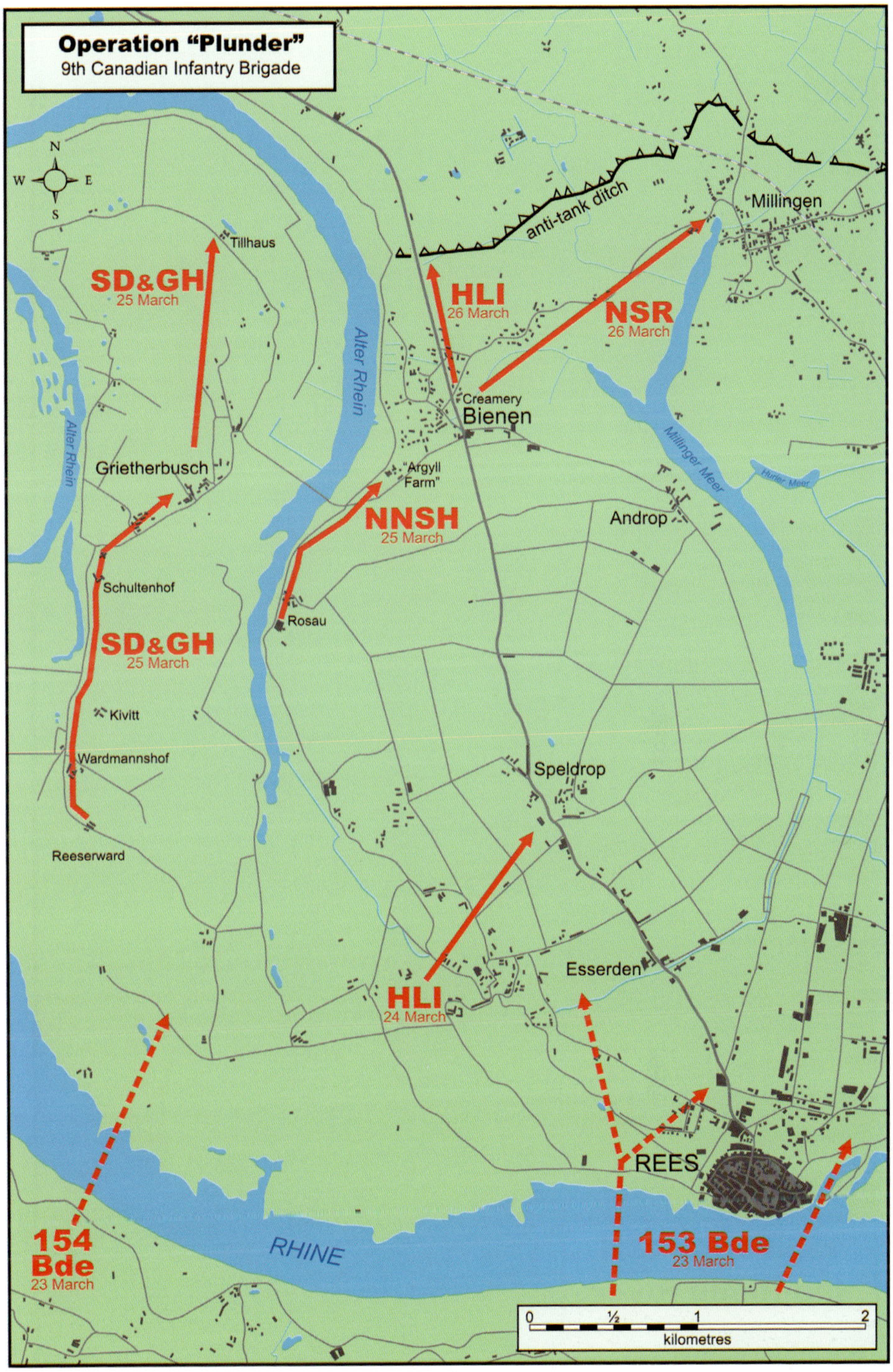

One strongpoint, made up of three fortified houses, defied the best efforts of the Regina Rifles and even Wasp flamethrowers could not force a surrender. The buildings were set on fire, but "it was not until plenty of grenades had been thrown down cellars that some 50-odd enemy…gave up." The Canadian Scottish Regiment also faced determined resistance crossing the Landwehr canal in the city centre

Two surviving Duplex Drive Sherman tanks pass the third of their troop "brewed-up" by a mine south of Speldrop, 24 March 1945. The Essex Yeomanry, equipped with DD Shermans, supported Scottish and Canadian units during the intial stages of Operation "Plunder."
LAC PA 190847

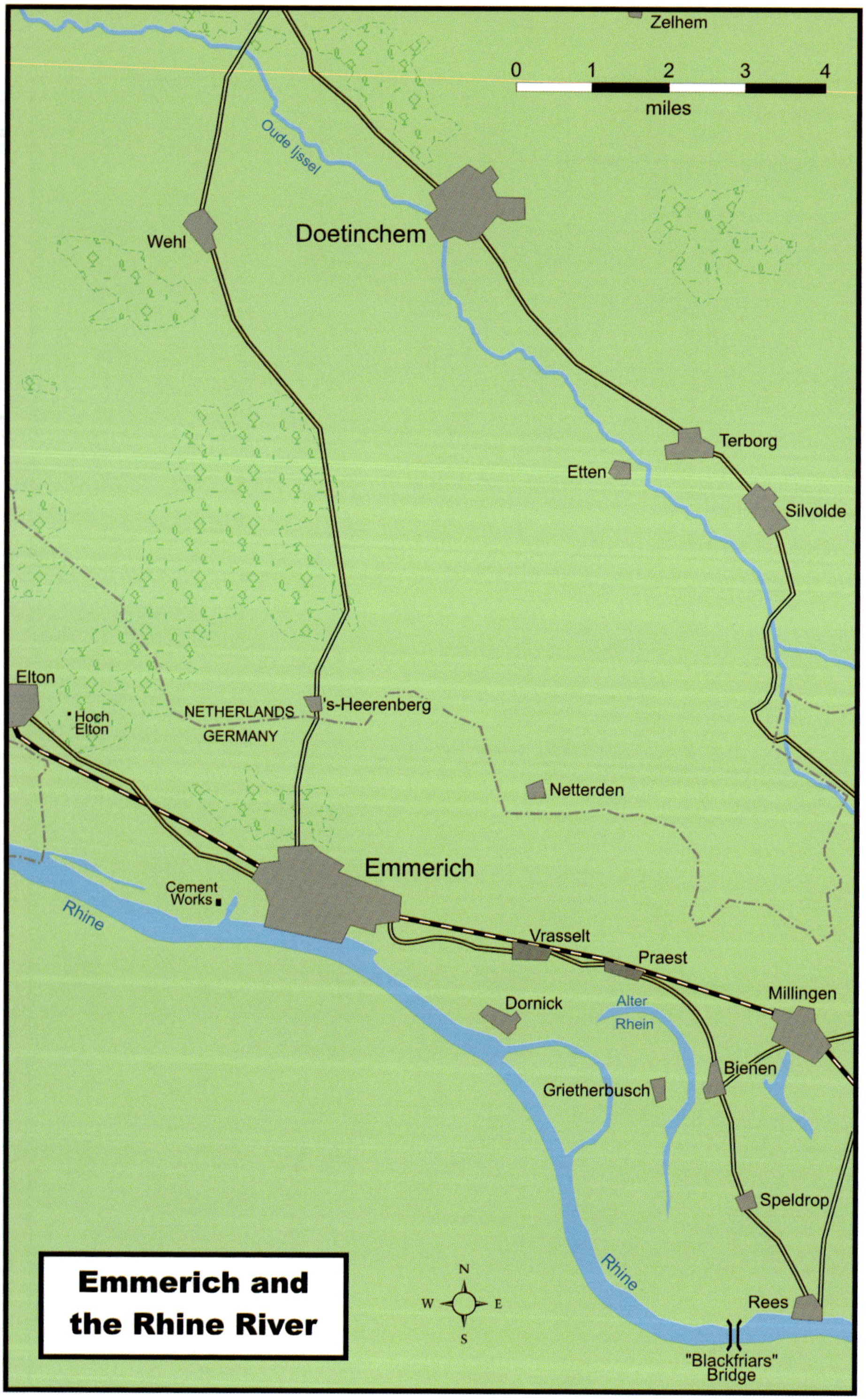

Emmerich and the Rhine River

General H.D.G. Crerar, Commander of First Canadian Army and General Dwight D. Eisenhower, Supreme Allied Commander Europe.
LCMSDS Photo Collection

while the Royal Winnipeg Rifles had to deal with a sharp counterattack before control of the quarter was established. By nightfall the Canscots had occupied the cement works on the western edge of town: Emmerich was secure.

On 30 March General Simonds' 2nd Canadian Corps attacked north out of the Rhine bridgehead with 8th Brigade seizing the Hoch Elten feature northwest of Emmerich. The position, however, had been abandoned by the Germans after an intense artillery barrage. To the right of 3rd Division, General Matthews' 2nd Division had entered the bridgehead and was pressing forward with 6th Brigade across the Dutch border.

Back at the river the Royal Canadian Engineers built "Blackfriars Bridge," the longest Bailey bridge of the war – 1,814 feet in length:

> Work started on 26 March and was completed at noon on 28 March. The construction was done by 29, 30 and 31 Canadian Field Companies RCE…The sappers and British pioneers toiled by night as well as day, using artificial moonlight…whenever fog set in, the searchlight was moved to the bridge and its beam aimed directly along the structure.

The Battle for the Rhine was over.

* * * * *

The battles fought by Scottish and Canadian troops in the Rhine crossing were as difficult and costly as any in the experience of the two veteran divisions. The decision to stop and organize a set-piece attack instead of bridging the Rhine allowed Montgomery time to build up resources so that his armies could race to Berlin once the bridgehead battle was won. This reasoned, though debatable, command decision placed an enormous burden on the battalions used to attack an enemy that had ample time to create and camouflage strong defensive positions.

Ironically, Montgomery's plans for a rapid thrust to Berlin were frustrated when Eisenhower decided to advance through the centre of Germany

to meet the Soviet armies at the Elbe River. British protests were to no avail. Berlin already under attack from the east, was well within the Soviet zone of occupation and Eisenhower had no intention of sacrificing men for such an objective.

There were other reasons for Eisenhower's decision, including the growing antagonism of American senior officer towards Montgomery and his methods. Bradley and Patton had long challenged the priority assigned to Montgomery's operations and when the Ninth US Army commander added his voice to the protests, Eisenhower decided to reunite Ninth US Army with Bradley's Army Group. Montgomery, with his British and Canadian armies, was to clear the Netherlands and northern Germany and protect the American flank, a very different task than the thrust to Berlin Montgomery had proposed.

* * * * *

Top: Vehicles cross "Blackfriars Bridge," the longest Bailey Bridge of the war. LAC PA 113687

Above centre: General Crerar, Field Marshal Alanbrooke, Chief of the Imperial General Staff, Lieutenant-General Guy Simonds, commander of 2nd Canadian Corps, Prime Minister Winston Churchill and Field Marshal Bernard L. Montgomery visit the Rhineland, 4 March 1945. CFJIC PMR 88-071

Right: Churchill is enthusiastically greeted by Canadian soldiers in the Hochwald area, 4 March 1945. Montgomery, with his distinctive two-badge beret, can be seen behind Churchill. LAC PA 145742

The Tour

We use Arnhem as a base for touring the Rhineland battles of February-March 1945 as well as the "Market Garden" battlefields. If you are following our suggested itinerary the drive from Kapelsche Veer to Arnhem will take about two hours. Follow the signs to "Centrum" (centre) and the railway station if you are staying in the centre of the city.

Once you are settled in the Arnhem area there is a great deal to do and see and you may have to make some tough choices. We begin with a full day devoted to Operation "Market Garden" and the Arnhem battlefields of September 1944. Start your tour at the Airborne Museum in Oosterbeek <www.airbornemuseum.com> which is situated in the Hartenstein Hotel, the headquarters of 1st Airborne Division. The Airborne Memorial and the Military Cemetery are nearby. If you wish to tour the entire battlefield there are excellent guide books available at the Museum store and at the Dutch Tourism Office (VVV) located beside the train station and opposite the Haarhuis Hotel in Arnhem. Canadians should make a special effort to visit the memorial to the Royal Canadian Engineers who were responsible for the final evacuation of troops across the Rhine. (See page 16 for a map and more details about this memorial.)

On day two we begin at the Canadian Military Cemetery at Groesbeek which includes a memorial listing the names of Canadian soldiers who have no known grave. The nearby National Liberation Museum <www.bevrijdingsmuseum.nl> introduces Operation "Veritable" but the main exhibit is on the role of US 82nd Airborne Division which liberated nearby Nijmegen in Operation "Market Garden." The museum includes a memorial hall with the names of all Allied soldiers killed in action in Northwest Europe.

Drive towards Wyler, the village captured by the Calgary Highlanders and Maisonneuves in the first hours of "Veritable," and look for the

John Frost Bridge (John Frostbrug) in Arnhem. This is the bridge captured by Lieutenant-Colonel John Frost's 2nd Parachute Battalion during Operation "Market Garden" (an episode which is vividly recreated in the movie "A Bridge Too Far.") This current bridge was built after the war, in the same pattern as the wartime bridge, after Allied bombing destroyed the original following the failed operation. This photo was taken from the tower of the Eusebius Church (Eusebiuskerk) in the centre of Arnhem. The elevator trip to the top of the 93 metre tower is worth the few Euro admission charge, but it is not for those who are afraid of heights!

stainless steel cairn which marks the startline for the operation. From here you can look across to the Reichswald Forest. Continue to Wyler and enter Germany. The villages on the left flank, which were cleared by the "Water Rats" of the 3rd Canadian Division, are still there but the flood waters are gone and so is the 1945 battlefield. Drive to Kranenburg and follow the signs to Kleve. The town was completely destroyed by bombing and artillery as part of the "Veritable" plan. It has been rebuilt as a handsome modern town good for lunch or shopping. Continue east on the N57 towards Kalkar and on your left you will see Moyland Castle, the home of Ann of Cleves. It is now an art museum <www.bedburg-hau.de/moyland/1-e.htm> but in 1944 the Maisonneuves made themselves at home here after the battle for Moyland Wood. Turn right and park at the first obvious turnoff on the right which is close to the startline for the Regina Rifles who tried to clear the sector along the highway with the Canscots on their right. You will have no difficulty in understanding why this wood was so difficult to clear. The Royal Winnipeg Rifles successful attack began from the east-west road, K27, south of the woods. The Little Black Devils counted Moyland as one of their most successful attacks of the war reflecting the high morale and outstanding leadership of the battalion.

Fourth Brigade's struggle to control the Goch-Kalkar road as a start line for a new set-piece attack was as difficult a battle as Moyland Wood. Follow the road from the village square at Louisendorf to the Goch-Kalkar road and you are on the brigade centre line. It takes some imagination to turn this featureless farm land back into a battlefield. The

Far left: The Groesbeek Canadian War Cemetery.

Left: Stainless steel cairn, on the Wylerbaan between Wyler and Groesbeek, which marks the startline of Operation "Veritable."

Right: A Canadian armoured car approaches the Xanten town gate, 22 March 1945.
LCMSDS Photo Collection

Below: The same gate, photographed from the rear, as it appears today.

Right: A Sherman tank belonging to the Sherbrooke Fusiliers passes the ruins of a windmill in Xanten, 7 March 1945.
LAC PA 114966

Far right: The same restored windmill as it now appears.

courageous infantry held the ground but it was the guns and the FOOs who directed their fire at the German counterattacks that won the battle.

When Canadian operations resumed on 26 February the new set-piece attack known as "Blockbuster" was launched from the Goch-Kalkar road. There are few signs of the horrific battles waged here and we usually drive slowly to the edge of the Hochwald. The parking area at the Schmachdarm is in the area where 2nd Division entered the forest and where Major Fred Tilston won the Victoria Cross. Continue south on the K4 to Üdemerbruch where the South Alberta Regimental Association has placed a plaque in memory of the battle for the Hochwald Gap. Be sure and visit the Villa Reichswald for coffee or a beer and a clear view of the gap. The high ground of Point 73 is to the west of the Villa and may be seen from the garden. Looking east on a clear day the church tower in Xanten is visible. The railway line is now a walking trail.

Many of those who help guide our tours think the Rhineland deserves more attention than we give it but the reality is few people know very much about this phase of the war and there is consequently less interest in what happened here.

From the Villa Reichswald it is a short drive to Xanten. Xanten is also the location of a Roman Amphitheatre and archaeological park which is of great interest to many visitors. Dr. Ralph Trost, an historian who is a native of Xanten, has written an interesting account of the impact of the war on the area. He introduced us to the crypt in the Xanten Catherdral with its memorial to the Holocaust.

On our tours we take a day to visit the National War and Resistance Museum at Overloon or the Kröller-Müller Art Gallery <www.kmm.nl>. The Overloon museum <www.oorlogsmuseum-overloon.nl> is located on the site of a battle fought by Second British Army in the aftermath of

Above: The Dutch National War and Resistance Museum at Overloon features an excellent collection including a large outdoor display of tanks and other vehicles that were abandoned following a battle fought on the site of the future museum. This Sherman tank was hit by numerous armour-piercing shells which, among other damage, dislodged the tank's turret.

Left: The Rhine River near Rees where 9th Canadian Infantry Brigade crossed during Operation "Plunder." This photo captures the rainstorm sweeping down the river.

Left: A memorial in the churchyard at Bienen which remembers the soldiers who died during the battle, both Canadian and German. The plaque reads:

This tablet has been placed by a group of surviving Canadian veterans of the North Nova Scotia Highlanders, 3 Canadian Infantry Division, in proud and grateful memory of those 40 members of their regiment who fell in battle at Bienen, Germany on Sunday March 25, 1945 and in memory of those fellow combatants of 9 Canadian Infantry (Highland) Brigade and 51 British Highland Division who died in the same battle and in the same cause and, as well, in respectful memory of those adversaries of the German army who died on that same day.

Photos by Robb Furlong

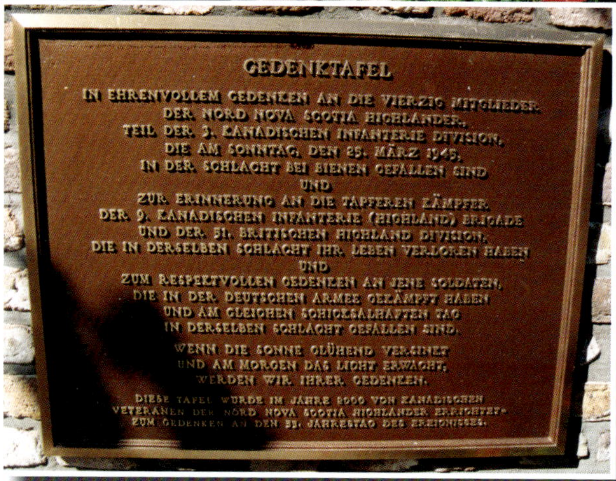

"Market Garden." Many of the damaged armoured vehicles and guns on display here were recovered from this battlefield. There is much else to see including displays depicting the occupation of Holland, the Holocaust, and the liberation of the country.

The largest Commonwealth War Cemetery in the area is located south of Cleve. General Crerar insisted that all Canadian soldiers killed in Germany be brought to Grosbeek or Holten, but 706 Canadian airmen as well and many British are buried in the Reichswald and at a second Rhineland cemetery near Rheinberg.

We return to the Rhineland to examine the Rhine crossing from a vantage point on the south bank near the place where 9th Canadian Brigade, then under the command of 51st Highland Division, crossed the river. All those who were with us on our 2001 tour will recall historian Lee

The high feature at Hoch Elton offers a panoramic view of the surrounding countryside, all the way to Emmerich (visible at top of photo).

Photo by Evert Stieber

Airfield B.88

You may wish to make one detour to the village of Nistelrode. Exit 16 off the A50 on the east side of S'Hertogenbosch. This was the site of B.88, the 2nd Tactical Air Force airfield assigned to RCAF 126 Fighter Wing, made up of the senior Canadian fighter squadron 401 (Ram), along with 411 (Grizzly Bear) and 412 (Falcon) squadrons. B.88 was the airfield where Flight Lieutenant Richard Audet was based when he shot down five enemy aircraft on a single mission on 29 December 1944. This was a feat unequalled by any other pilot in the RCAF or in 2nd TAF. Altogether, the Wing accounted for 11 aircraft that day. For his actions Audet was awarded the Distinguished Flying Cross. On January 1st, when the Luftwaffe flew more than 1,000 sorties in the famous "hangover raid," 126 Wing was able to get 401 Squadron airborne quickly and during the day 19 enemy aircraft were shot down while damage to B.88 and its aircraft was limited to a hole in the dispersal tent. The citizens of Nistelrode-Heesch have created a strikingly beautiful memorial to the Canadian pilots killed-in-action while serving at B.88. R.J. Audet, killed on 3 March 1945, is one of the 14 names inscribed on stone blocks surrounding a coloured mosaic of a poppy. B.88 was on the north edge of Nistelrode. The Noorderbaan crosses the main runway and "Canada Baan" is at the south end. The memorial is in the town centre across from the church.

Flight Lieutenant Richard Audet, DFC & bar
CFJIC PL41716

Windsor describing the crossings as a localized but very heavy rainstorm swept towards us down the river. He was not willing to concede to Mother Nature and began to speak faster, trying to finish his briefing before the storm sent people running for cover. Mother Nature won. The viewing point is at the end of the Reeserschanz road off the L8 just east of Highway 67 and the bridge to Rees.

Cross the Rhine and take Highway N8 towards Wesel. There is a parking area just before the 6th British Airborne drop zones for Operation "Varsity." First Canadian Parachute Battalion landed beside the N8 in the open area immediately north of the woods. Follow the N8 north to Emmerich and Hoch Elten. The battles for Emmerich and the villages on the north bank of the Rhine are very difficult to retrace as the necessary re-building, extensive urbanization and the changing shape of the river have altered much of the landscape. "Blackfriars Bridge" was almost exactly where the new bridge crosses the Rhine at Rees. Ninth Brigade crossed the river north of the "yachthafen" moving cross-country to Bienen and Millingen. The churchyard in Bienen is the site of plaques dedicated to the memory of the Canadian, British and German soldiers killed in the battles for the village. Seventh Brigade then advanced down the N8 to Emmerich, while the 2nd Division started north with the two divisional Recce Regiments maintaining contact.

The cement works so prominent in the battle for Emmerich were beside the yachthafen. Emmerich itself was completely devastated by bombing. The Hoch Elten, a wooded ridge overlooking the Rhine was subjected to one of the heaviest artillery programs of the war because enemy troops there could interfere with the engineers bridging the Rhine. The men of the 8th Canadian Infantry Brigade captured the feature without too much difficulty.

The Dutch border is now just a few kilometres away so it is time to turn your attention to the events of April 1945 and the liberation of the Netherlands.

Another site worth visiting is the Reichswald Forest War Cemetery. There are 7,594 Commonwealth servicemen of the Second World War buried or commemorated in this cemetery. It is the largest Commonwealth cemetery in Germany and it is the final resting place of many soldiers who were killed in the Rhineland campaign as well as Allied airmen, primarily bomber crew, who were shot down over western Germany.

The Liberation of the Netherlands

On 28 March Field Marshal Montgomery declared, "we have won the battle of the Rhine." He went on to urge his commanders to exploit the new situation as quickly as possible. First Canadian Army was to "open up the supply route to the north through Arnhem and then to clear Northeast Holland, the coastal belt (of Germany) towards the Elbe and West Holland."

First Canadian Army would undertake these tasks without 4th Division which was to protect the left flank of the British advance to Bremen and Hamburg. Second Division advanced to Groningen while 3rd Division moved due north to Leeuwarden. First Polish Armoured Division was brought out of reserve to fill the gap between 2nd Division's northerly axis and 4th Division's north-eastern route. Western Holland was assigned to 1st Canadian Corps which had arrived from Italy in March via Marseilles and the Rhône Valley. The "D-Day Dodgers," as the veterans of the Italian campaign jokingly called themselves, were to follow up the capture of Arnhem, assigned to 49th (West Riding) Division, with a thrust to Apeldoorn. Thereafter, 1st Corps would move west towards the old provinces of Holland and the cities of Rotterdam and Amsterdam.

These operations which began on 2 April included some short, sharp encounters which are examined in the following sections. However, it is important to note the general characteristics of the April campaign first. In purely military terms, April was a month of anti-climax. The 4th Division was involved in a tough battle at the Twente Canal near Delden on 2 April, but 12 days later, it had advanced almost 100 miles to the Küsten Canal without serious difficulty. Second Division was at the outskirts of Groningen on 13 April and 3rd Division's 7th Recce Regiment, met 1st Canadian Armoured Car Regiment (The Royal Canadian Dragoons), in Leeuwarden on 16 April. In 1st Corps' sector, fighting ceased on 19 April,

Holten Canadian War Cemetery, Christmas Eve 2004.
Photo by Evert Stieber

The "sweetest of springs" Dutch girls walk arm-in-arm with Canadian soldiers in Harderwijk, Netherlands, 19 April 1945.
LAC PA 133152

when the decision was made to halt operations to deal with famine conditions in the occupied Netherlands.

If the story of Canadian operations in April contains no great decisive battles, it includes a potent mix of both triumph and tragedy. Canadian and Dutch memories of April are usually recollections of that "sweetest of springs," the spring of liberation. Canadian soldiers found themselves engulfed by a joyous population which knew, all too well, what the war had been fought for, and they showered their liberators with kisses and flowers and love. But April was also the cruellest month; while the war had been won, the killing did not stop.

Fatal casualties are often the best measure of the intensity of combat. For the Canadians in northwest Europe, the worst days had been 6 June with 359 fatalities; 8 July (262); 25 July (344); 8 August (290); 14 August (261); and 26 February (214). On 16 other days, many of them in October 1944, fatalities exceeded 100 men. The last such 100-fatality day was 10 March 1945 at Xanten and Veen. In April 1945 more than 50 soldiers were killed on each of seven days; 114 more were killed between 1 May and the surrender on 5 May, including 12 on the last day of fighting in Europe.

This tragic toll in young men's lives took place against a background of the triumphant defeat of the Nazi menace, but the victory was achieved at great cost.

3rd Division

Zutphen, Deventer and Leeuwarden

Third Canadian Division had started north on 3 April, but 7th Brigade soon ran into resistance in the village of Wehl. This position was overcome by a pincer attack carried out by the Regina Rifles. From Wehl 3rd Division advanced towards Zutphen, a town on the Ijssel River at the end of the Twente Canal.

Ninth Brigade was in the lead when strong resistance was encountered at Warnsveld. The North Novas ran into a well-organized position based on a hospital. The defenders were using a dual 20 mm gun as an extra heavy machine gun, and the regiment pulled back until two troops of Crocodiles were available and a new attack organized. After this resistance was overcome the North Novas, Glens and HLI pressed forward on a three-battalion front with vital support from tanks of the Sherbrooke Fusiliers. Prisoners taken were described as "young, about sixteen and seventeen years of age…when interviewed they still thought Germany would win and their belief in Hitler and Nazism was still unshaken. However, there were cases among the prisoners of just badly scared boys."

Brigadier J.A. Roberts' 8th Brigade began the task of clearing Zutphen. The attack was made from the east with the North Shores and Chaudières forced into a difficult exercise in street fighting against a determined garrison which included young officer cadets from a Luftwaffe paratrooper school. The defences of Zutphen were well prepared with the bridges down and anti-tank obstacles blocking the roads. To win the day, the infantry and engineers had to fill the bridge gaps and clear a path for the tanks of the Sherbrooke Fusiliers and the attached Crocodiles.

A Chaudière lieutenant described the two-day encounter in terms which stress the character of German resistance:

> Between the start line and the objective, there was a canal on which both leading companies stopped for almost two hours…[because of] well-sited snipers, MG nests and bazookas. All enemy positions were dealt with by proper use of infantry on ground supported by tank fire…the enemy which we had to fight were often first class troops and have shown a bitter fighting spirit…when they did surrender it was because they were out of ammunition or deprived of any escape.

Zutphen was not completely clear until the afternoon of April 8th.

The next day, 3rd Division moved on to the Schipbeek Canal and the city of Deventer. Again the Germans had dug in behind a water barrier and 7th Brigade was ordered to cross the canal quickly as preparation for an attack on Deventer from the east. Both the Royal Winnipeg Rifles and the Canadian Scottish were required to undertake a daylight attack without much knowledge of the extent of enemy strength or dispositions. The Winnipegs were stunned by the intensity of the German fire, but they had the Sherbrooke tanks and Crocodiles with them. More than 200 prisoners were taken on the outskirts of town and, after a bulldozer had filled in a passage across the anti-tank ditch, the armour made quick work of the remaining enemy.

The Canadian Scottish had an easier time on the north edge of the town as the defenders here seemed ready to retreat quickly once the Crocodiles appeared. Nevertheless, one platoon commander and four other ranks were killed with 22 wounded in the approach and subsequent clearing of the town.

The Canscot War Diary provides an interesting commentary on the role of the Dutch resistance at Deventer:

Sherman tanks from the Sherbrooke Fusiliers along side a canal outside of Deventer, Holland, 10 April 1945.
LAC PA 136173

...It would have been impossible to take and hold the town of Deventer so successfully if it had not been for the splendid cooperation of the Dutch Underground Movement. There was a continuous stream of German PW and civilian prisoners being brought in to the Command Post for dispatch to the PW cage. It is impossible to describe fully the enthusiasm with which the people of Deventer welcomed the battalion. No member of the battalion could stop on the street without having a flock of men, women and children gather around him asking for chocolate and cigarettes as an introduction to any other conversation they might have to offer. It was learned that the occupation of Deventer by this battalion would come to a rapid end this afternoon. The troops were not pleased with this news as we had hoped to have a day or so amongst the friendly people.

Opposite top: Soldiers of "C" Company, North Shore Regiment crossing the Berkel River into Zutphen, 7 April 1945. LAC PA 130059

Opposite middle: The same location as it appears today. Photo by Evert Stieber

Opposite bottom: The rebuilt bridge is now known as "Canadians' Bridge." The plaque on the bridge states: "April 8th 1945 The Canadian troops liberated Zutphen entering by this road." Photo by Evert Stieber

There were other sharp encounters. The Glens, for example, secured a bridgehead across the Overijssel Canal, north of Heino and then had to fight off an attack which included artillery and some armour. Lieutenant-Colonel N.W. Gemmell told the Historical Officer that:

> The anti-tank guns, Wasps and Carriers were on the wrong side of the canal when the attack started. The Second-in-Command collected a force of drivers, snipers, cooks and batmen who, despite the enemy fire, manhandled the 6-pounders over the canal. The crews dismantled the .50 Browning machine guns from the carriers. With these and the ammunition for the guns, they piled into the one and only jeep and raced to a forward position…In less than one hour the guns were over the canal…The artillery fire was not all one-sided…Within a matter of a few seconds the Artillery C.O.'s Rep. was bringing down fire within 50 yards.

This was the last major obstacle on the road to Leeuwarden. The divisional recce unit, the 17th Duke of York's Royal Canadian Hussars, got the opportunity to race ahead and reached the town on 15 April. The war was not, however, quite over for 3rd Division. The last week of April and the first week of May were to be spent in Germany and all too often there would be nasty little battles which, to the ordinary soldier, made less and less sense as each day passed.

1st Division

The Ijssel Bridgehead and Apeldoorn

The operations of 3rd Canadian Division during the first week of April were closely tied to the task of 1st Canadian Corps in the struggle to capture Arnhem, re-bridge the Rhine and open a major maintenance route for both the Canadian and British armies. The battle for Arnhem was the responsibility of 49th Division. 1st British Corps, which had served under General Crerar's command since 23 July 1944, had rejoined Second British Army when 1st Canadian Corps arrived from Italy, but the West Riding Division was left in place to undertake a revised version of Operation "Wallstreet."

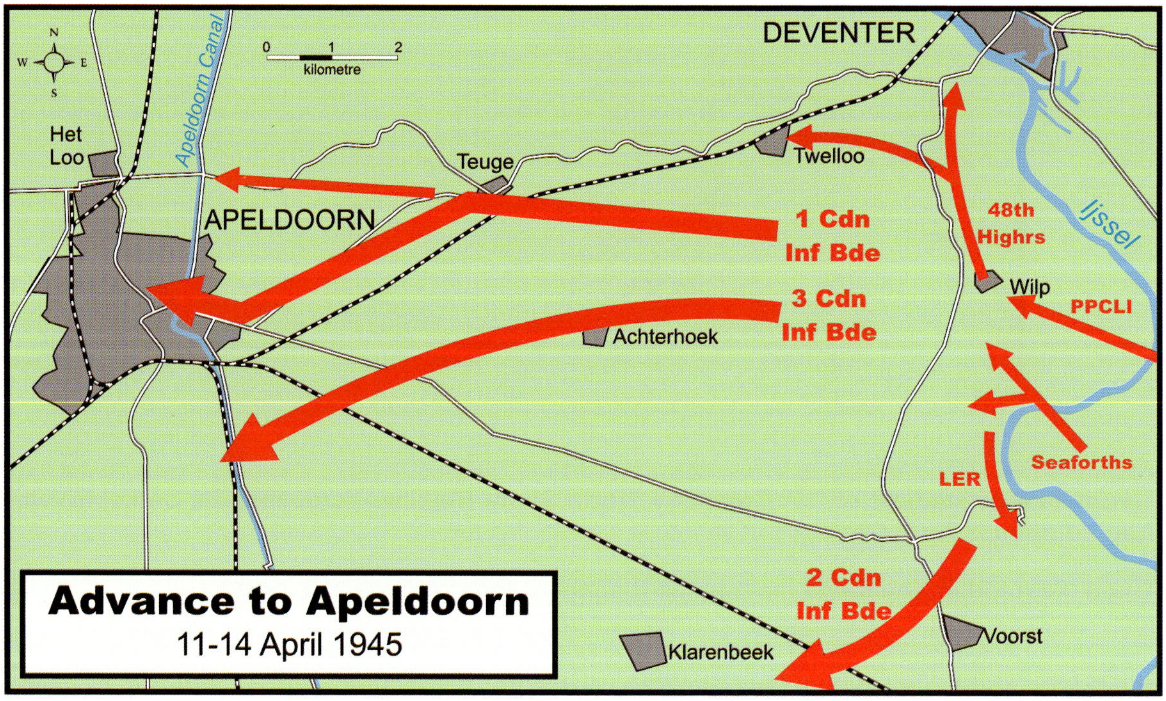

The first task was to clear the "island" between Nijmegen and Arnhem, an area the regiments of 49th Division knew thoroughly from months of patrols. The Ontario Regiment of 1st Canadian Armoured Brigade provided the tank support for this operation which began on 2 April. The 49th Division was also assisted by the 11th Canadian Infantry Brigade which cleared the left flank as the British advanced.

The army commander, General Harry Crerar, decided to delay a direct attack on Arnhem until the city and its defenders were cut off by an advance across the Ijssel River to Apeldoorn. This in turn depended upon the success of 3rd Canadian Division in clearing the east bank of the river and the cities of Zutphen and Deventer. As the Canadians prepared for these operations they were confronted with a new set of problems. Reports from the old provinces of Holland, including the cities of Amsterdam and Rotterdam, indicated that the terrible conditions of the "hunger winter" were continuing and the people of western Holland were facing starvation. The Nazi governor, Arthur Seyss-Inquart, had deliberately created the food shortage in retaliation for the actions of the Dutch resistance and now threatened to flood much of Holland as a defensive measure. If military action was the answer, all possible speed was required.

First Division, waiting in the Rhineland, was placed under the command of Guy Simonds' 2nd Canadian Corps. Formation patches and divisional signs were removed and the division was brought north to woods in the vicinity of Gorssel while 3rd Division captured Zutphen. Major-General Harry Foster held his "O" group on 10 April and outlined the plan for the first phase of Operation "Cannonshot." Foster selected 2nd Canadian Infantry Brigade (The Princess Patricia's Canadian Light Infantry, The Seaforth Highlanders of Canada, The Loyal Edmonton Regiment) to make the assault crossing of the Ijssel River.

Each brigade in 1st Division had one battalion from a Permanent Force regiment and two militia battalions. This distinction had been of some importance during training in England but by 1945 very few officers and non-commissioned officers who served in the early years of the war were still around and the battalions were staffed with the products of Brockville and other officer training schools, while many senior NCOs were former privates. This citizen army had acquired a high degree of professionalism, particularly at the staff level and in the supporting arms. Infantry rifle companies suffered such high casualties that the ever-changing mix of officers and NCOs makes generalization about comparative combat effectiveness impossible. A battalion that distinguished itself in 1944 might still carry the same proud name in 1945 but it was made of different men. Sydney Frost, a captain in the Patricias during Operation "Cannonshot," noted that just two officers who had landed with the Patricias in Sicily were still with the battalion in April 1945. Despite the turnover regimental traditions and reputations lived on.

Major-General Harry Foster, commander of 1st Canadian Infantry Division. He is shown here as a Brigadier in late 1943-early 1944 when he commanded 13th Canadian Infantry Brigade during the Kiska invasion. The blue badge on his shoulder is known as the "Kiska Patch" and was worn by all Canadian and American personnel who took part in that operation.
CFJIC ZK 444

The 2nd Canadian Infantry Brigade had long been considered the outstanding brigade in the Canadian army. During his famous 1942 inspection, Montgomery, declared that the 2nd could be the best brigade in all the Commonwealth armies. "The PPCLI," he wrote, "have the best officers, the Seaforths the best NCOs and the Edmontons the best men." After Sicily and Ortona

Top: This air photo, taken from the east, shows where the Seaforth Highlanders of Canada crossed the Ijssel River on 11 April 1945.

Right: Location where the PPCLI crossed the Ijssel River, as seen from the west. The village of Gorssel is visible at the top left and the road in the upper left leads to Zutphen.

Below: Monument to the Canadians at Gorssel. The plaque states, "With the crossing the of Ijssel at Gorssel on 12 April 1945 [sic] the liberation of the West Netherlands started."

Photos by Evert Stieber

and the promotion of Brigadiers Chris Vokes and Bert Hoffmeister to divisional commands, the reputation of the 2nd Brigade was set for all time. One result was that it got more than its share of high profile operations.

Brigadier M.P. Bogert, a veteran of the Italian Campaign, was now in command and he planned the assault crossing within the framework of Brigadier Stanley Todd's Corps artillery fire plan. The battalions were introduced to the Buffalo, a Landing Vehicle Tracked, which could enter and leave the water on most gradients while providing 30 men with protection from small arms fire. The corps plan called for an elaborate "smoke box" created by smoke generators and concentrations of medium and heavy artillery on prearranged targets with virtually unlimited artillery on call down to company level. Medium bombers were to hit prearranged targets and Typhoon aircraft were on call. This was war in a new style for those who had fought in Italy. In his memoirs, *Once A Patricia*, Syd Frost writes: "The more I saw of the orderly, deliberate way the Canadian Army (in Northwest Europe) went about its tasks, the more I liked doing business with them."

Operation "Cannonshot," was launched at 1530 hours on 11 April. The enemy appeared to be totally surprised. Apparently ignorant of 1st Division's presence they assumed that the attack would come from 3rd Division at Deventer. The initial opposition came from small German battlegroups built around one or two self-propelled guns. The Seaforths and PPCLI used their PIATs (Projector, Infantry, Anti-Tank) until the first anti-tank guns got across the river. By 2100 hours the bridgehead was "snug." German reserves reached the area at midnight and in accordance with their doctrine counterattacked immediately.

Military historians have long argued that the German army was particularly effective on the battlefields of World War II because of its training and commitment to mission tactics. The German army's *Instructions On The Command of Troops* insisted that "decisive action remains the prerequisite for success in war. Everybody from the highest commander to the youngest soldier must be conscious of the fact that inactivity and lost opportunities weigh heavier than do errors in the choice of means." In other words, if in doubt, attack. Perhaps this doctrine has merits in the abstract but the Allies had long since learned that German battlefield behaviour was amazingly predictable. That is why competent Allied commanders insisted on digging-in after an assault rather than exploiting their initial success. Why, they reasoned, risk an encounter battle when the enemy will come to you allowing your artillery,

There is a small memorial on the wall of the church in Wilp to Lieutenant-Colonel D.A. Mackenzie, commanding officer of the 48th Highlanders, who was killed on 12 April 1945. The plaque says, "To the memory of the 48th Highlanders of Canada. 19 Highlanders fell in and around the villageship of Voorst, including the commanding officer.
Photos by Evert Stieber

mortars and machine-guns to destroy them with observed fire?

This is precisely what happened in the Ijssel bridgehead. The Seaforths and PPCLI repulsed hastily-mounted counterattacks, taking more than 200 prisoners and inflicting heavy casualties. The Loyal Eddies joined them, and by dawn the engineers had a bridge in place and the tanks of the First Hussars were across in preparation for the next phase.

The plan now called for Brigadier J.D.B. Smith's 1st Canadian Infantry Brigade (Royal Canadian Regiment, 48th Highlanders, Hastings and Prince Edward Regiment) to advance east along the axis of the Apeldoorn-Deventer railway to the airfield at Teague while Brigadier J.P.E. Bernatchez's 3rd Canadian Infantry Brigade (Royal 22e Régiment, Carleton and York Regiment and West Nova Scotia Regiment) was directed south of Apeldoorn to prepare an assault crossing of the canal in the event 1st Brigade ran into difficulty.

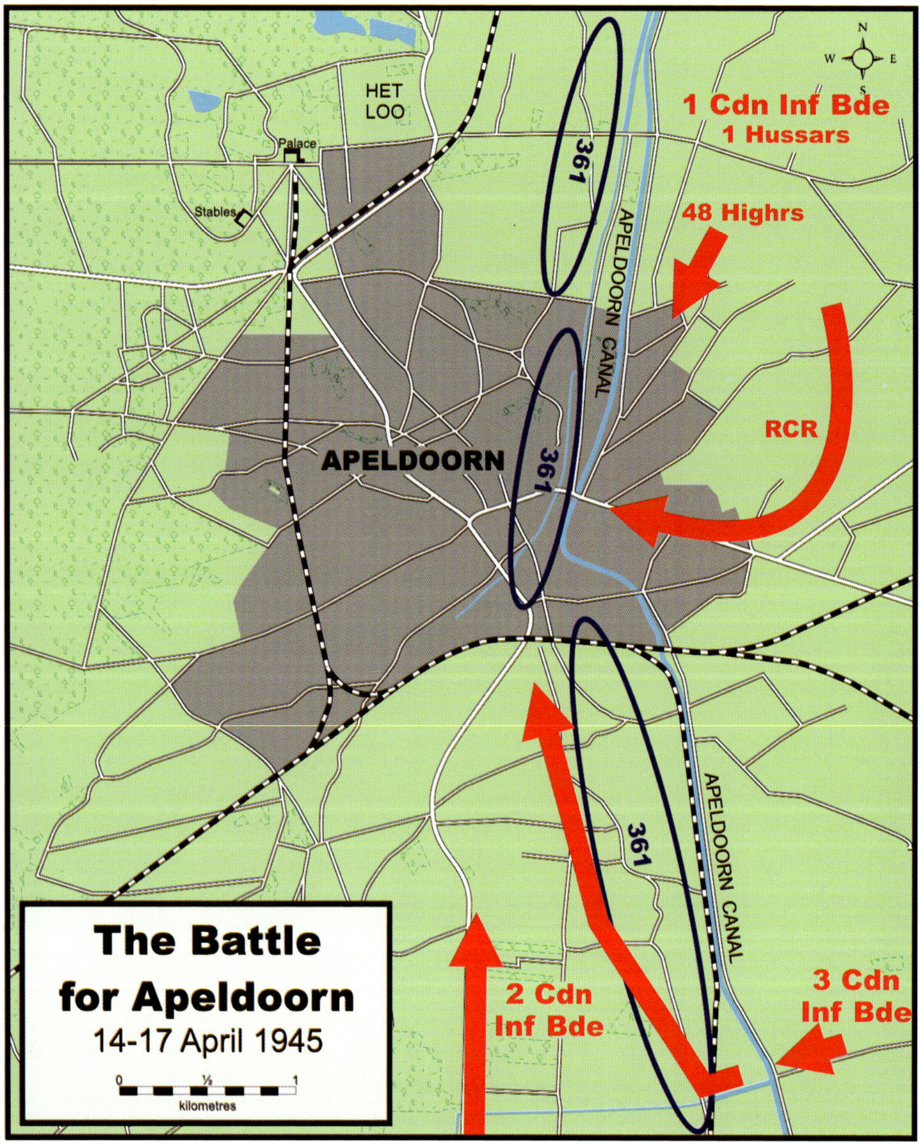

With the 48th Highlanders leading, 1st Brigade moved swiftly west. Resistance was spotty but one burst of shell fire struck the command group killing Lieutenant-Colonel D.A. Mackenzie, the Highlanders' commanding officer. The RCR (Lieutenant-Colonel D.A. Reid) with "C" Squadron of the First Hussars took over the lead and by noon on the 13th were less than one mile from Apeldoorn. The plan to pause at the airfield and prepare a co-ordinated attack across the Apeldoorn canal north of the city was abandoned when the Dutch resistance reported that the main road bridge over the canal, in the heart of the city, was intact. At first light on the 14th the RCR-First Hussar battlegroup fought its way toward the bridge which turned out to be well protected by anti-tank guns. The Hussars lost two tanks, including one which tried to smash through a road block. North of the city the bridges were blown and patrols from the Hasty Ps established that the canal was strongly defended.

To the south, 3rd Brigade was held up by a strong enemy position until Bernatchez ordered the lead battalions to bypass the resistance and head for the canal. The Royal 22e Régiment, as the reserve battalion, was ordered to deal with the enemy and did so by assaulting the woods from the rear. It then joined its sister battalions along the canal two kilometres south of Apeldoorn. It was now the evening of 15 April. "Cannonshot," which had begun with such great promise four days earlier, was in danger of deteriorating into a series of costly piecemeal attacks.

Major-General Harry Foster, commander of 1st Canadian Infantry Division, did nothing to help the situation when he ordered 1st Brigade to continue operations to attack across the canal in the centre of Apeldoorn. To the north and south of the city the enemy had created a thin crust of defences based on the western bank of the canal. A set-piece attack with the kind of assets used in the crossing of the much wider Ijssel would bring

Dutch children run out to greet Canadian troops as they pass through their village.
LAC PA 191310

certain success and force the enemy to abandon the city or risk encirclement. Fighting to clear city streets in a town full of friendly civilians and refugees was not a brilliant idea. No one could use tactical air or serious artillery fire against a Dutch city, so the infantry and tanks would have to do it one house at a time.

The RCR and 48th Highlanders went about their task carefully. With the BBC reporting that the Red Army was in the suburbs of Berlin and the Germans seeking a truce in western Holland, no one wanted to take unnecessary casualties in what appeared to be the last days of the war. The attack quickly turned into a stalemate. The forward companies were "pinned down by arty, mortar and machine-gun fire" and the supporting tanks were bogged down trying an indirect approach to the canal. A request for Crocodiles to flame the basements of houses along the canal was refused, as none were immediately available.

The best solution seemed to be an assault crossing of the canal south of the city by 3rd Brigade. Bernatchez was warned to plan such an attack but as divisional engineers and artillery prepared to provide support the situation suddenly changed. The army commander wanted bridges across the river at Zutphen, and ordered 2nd Brigade south. The Germans had abandoned the area because 5th Canadian Armoured Division had entered Arnhem and turned east, threatening to cut off the enemy. This manoeuvre allowed 2nd Brigade to do an unopposed crossing of the Apeldoorn Canal and then advance north, turning the enemy positions in front of 3rd Brigade. The Germans withdrew as fast as they could run, abandoning equipment and the city of Apeldoorn. Syd Frost recalls that, "The War Diarist of the Loyal Edmonton Regiment could not restrain his envy of the staff cars, vehicles, household wares, food and other loot left behind by the Germans for the Patricias: 'the PPCLI had been busy on our right capturing hundreds of wandering enemy with so much loot that most of the Patricias were offering to resign their positions as privates and go home to live in a manner befitting their status as millionaires.'" RCR patrols reported the enemy was gone and on 17 April the regiment was in the centre of the city.

The joy of the Dutch population knew no bounds. It had appeared as if their garden city was to become a battleground and now, almost miraculously, the fighting had ended. The war diarist of the Hastings and Prince Edward Regiment described the scene that followed:

> The battalion crossed the bridge and got formed up on the west side of the Canal, a brief Orders Group was held and we started through the city. It was tough going due to the cheering and crowding of the thousands of liberated Dutch people who crowded the streets and showered bouquets of flowers on the troops…many a fair maiden's kiss was forced on the boys.

Canadian veterans who return to Apeldoorn for the anniversaries of the liberation know that memories of 1945 are still warm. First Division suffered 506 casualties, more than 100 of them fatal, in the six days of Operation "Cannonshot." Most of 1st Brigade's 184 losses came in the fighting for Apeldoorn.

5th Division

Otterlo and Barneveld

Since their arrival in Holland Major-General B.M. Hoffmeister's 5th Armoured Division had been offered little opportunity to use their armoured brigade group. The relatively easy conquest of Arnhem had, however, presented the Corps Commander with an irresistible opportunity to use the 5th Armoured Brigade to cut off the retreat of the Germans still fighting on the Apeldoorn canal line. The British Columbia Dragoons led the way through Arnhem with the 8th Hussars, the Westminster Regiment (Motor) and the Lord Strathcona's Horse close behind. Enemy blocking positions were shot up or by-passed and Otterlo was reached by late afternoon.

Brigadier Cumberland was not about to pause. The Strathconas were told to take Otterlo then push on to capture Barneveld. If Barneveld was defended they were to bypass it and strike north to cut the Apeldoorn-Amersfoort road, the main east-west route of the retreating German forces. The other two armoured regiments were to conform to this thrust, the BCDs to the north and the 8th Hussars to the south. Otterlo was cleared readily enough, but beyond the town there were numerous pockets of infantry, some with *panzerfaust* (anti-tank weapons), who had to be dealt with by Westminster motorized infantry.

The enemy held Barneveld in strength and the Strathconas lost three tanks on the edge of town. Bypassing was accomplished quickly, but 2000 metres beyond the north edge of town a well-organized anti-tank gun position, guarded by machine gun posts, barred the way. The decision was made to stop and organize a proper attack at first light on the 17 April.

The night of 16-17 April is remembered as the Battle of Otterlo. The ferocious attack on the town, which included General Hoffmeister's advanced headquarters, was part of a determined attempt by elements of three German divisions to reach the "safety" of western Holland

The 11th Infantry Brigade had spent the two previous days following up the rapid moves of the 5th Armoured Brigade. By the evening of the 16

German prisoners and a Canadian medical orderly place a dead German soldier on a stretcher near Otterlo, Netherlands, 17 April 1945.
LAC PA 115441

General Harry Crerar confers with Major-General Bert Hoffmeister, 24 March 1945

LAC PA 134488

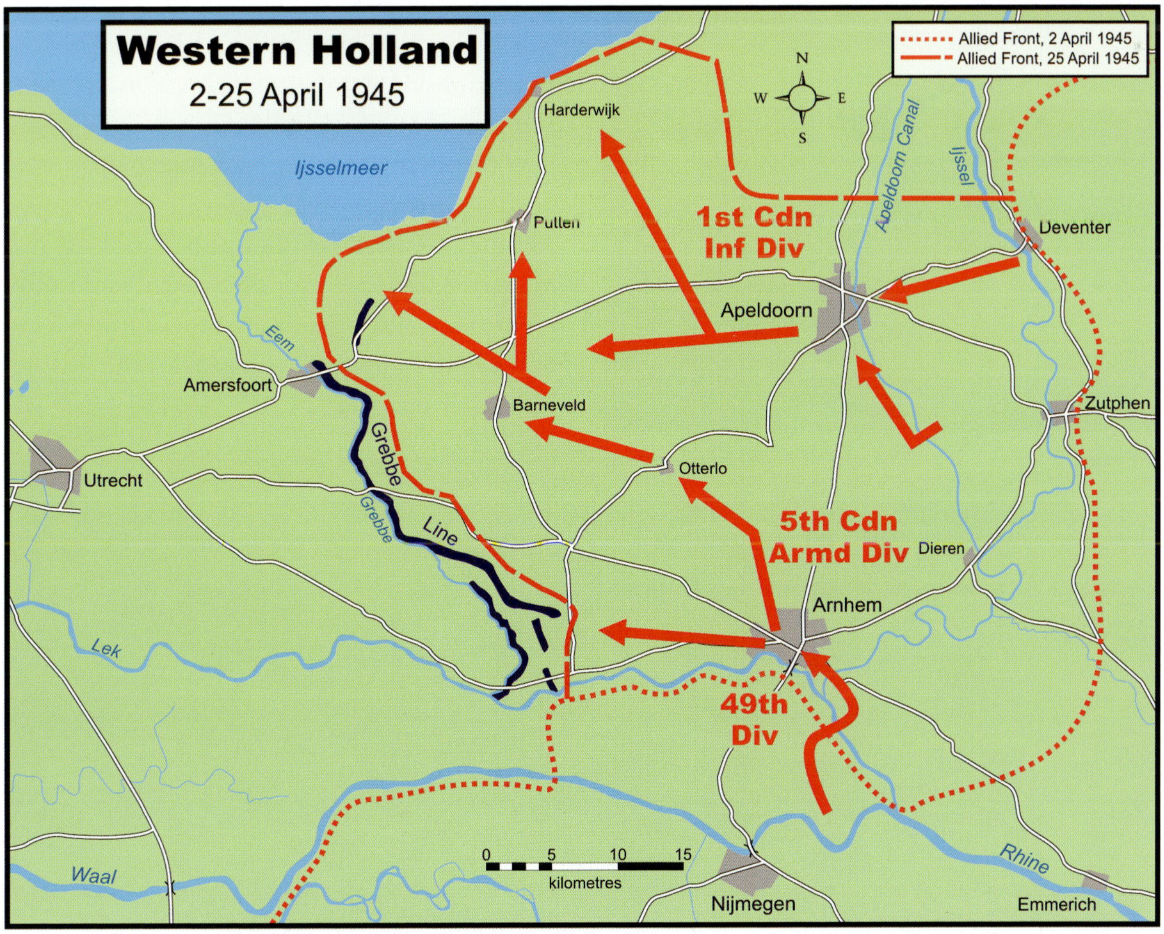

April the Irish Regiment of Canada was in Otterlo and General Hoffmeister placed it in position to control the north-eastern approaches to the town. The following account of the battle was given to the 5th Division Historical Officer by Lieutenant J. Hobson of Divisional Headquarters:

> The first enemy to appear were a strong fighting patrol who came in from the NE. These passed through the Irish position throwing grenades at the troops who were sleeping nearby...The attacking enemy were whooping and shouting in a very drunken manner...Mortar bombs were falling and Very Lights were being fired all about...The attacking force...next bumped into a troop of the 17th Field Regiment RCA...The gunners fought like mad. The Regiment SM shot two with a Sten and after it had jammed, he got another down and strangled him.
>
> ...The attacking force consisted of between five and six hundred second-rate troops...The force had come down from the neighbourhood of Apeldoorn via the main highway through Hoenderloo. Their task was to secure Otterlo and push on to the SW, concentrating at Ede. They had no choice but to come through Otterlo as they had strict orders to take all their transport and heavy equipment with them...

Below: A Sherman "Firefly" crosses a Bailey Bridge at the Twente Canal Locks, 4 April 1945.
LAC PA 130910

Bottom: Another Bailey Bridge over the Twente Canal near Zutphen.
LAC PA 145724

The enemy suffered more than 300 casualties in the chaotic encounter though some got through to the relative safety of the Grebbe Line.

The next day 5th Division was ready to continue their push west, but on the evening of 17 April a decision was made which would end the fighting in the western Netherlands. The desperate conditions in Holland during the "Hunger Winter" of 1944-45 had been bad enough, but now it appeared the Germans were preparing to flood vast stretches of the country to halt the Allied advance. General Eisenhower had decided that military operations west of Utrecht could serve no purpose and would only bring further harm to the long-suffering Dutch people. The decision to halt all operations at the "Grebbe Line" was

communicated to First Canadian Army on 19 April. For a brief moment 5th Division thought its war was over.

2nd Division

The Advance to Groningen

Second Division advanced north from the Rhine bridgehead on a one-brigade front with each brigade tasked to seize an objective and hold it while the next brigade passed through maintaining momentum. The Fort Garry Horse, the only available armoured regiment, was committed to support all three brigades. The first serious engagement took place at Doetinchem where the enemy fortified the centre of the town using cement-filled railway cars. The Calgary Highlanders employed Wasp flame throwers and the battalion 6-pounders to supplement the tanks but the town was not cleared until sappers from a Field Company of the Royal Canadian Engineers blew up the roadblocks. Calgary casualties, 6 killed and 41 wounded, were chilling evidence that elements of the German army were still committed to their cause. Doetinchem was the last action the Calgaries fought with their legendary CO Ross Ellis, who was ill, in command. Fortunately, Dalt Heyland who had commanded a Calgary company since Normandy took over the battalion maintaining the outstanding leadership that had helped to make the Calgary Highlanders one of the most effective battalions in the Allied armies.

Fourth Brigade was in the lead when the division reached the Twente Canal. Intelligence reports described the canal line as a major German defensive position but the Royal Regiment was able to rush the water barrier and establish a bridgehead in a well-organized attack. The RHLI joined the Royals north of the canal and the engineers moved quickly to build a bridge allowing the advance to continue with tank support.

No one has ever explained why the enemy defended the small town of Laren with such determination but when the Black Watch began to probe the defences

A Canadian convoy passes through Holten, 9 April 1945.
LAC PA 133178

A Canadian soldier poses beside the sign of the recently-liberated town of Groningen. LAC PA 130945

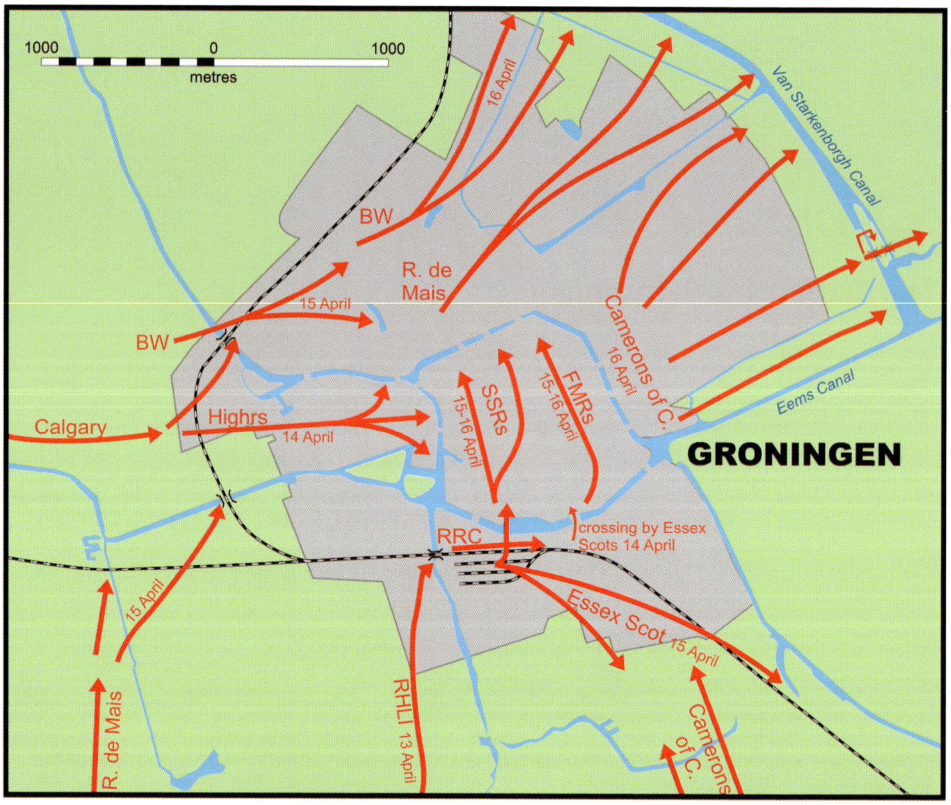

Above: Canadian tanks provide overwatch while the infantry clears buildings in Groningen, Netherlands, 16 April 1945. LAC PA 130992

Above right: Major-General Bruce Matthews, commander of 2nd Canadian Infantry Division. CFJIC ZK 948-1

it was evident that this time the defenders were supported by artillery and armour. The Black Watch suffered 42 casualties including 14 killed in a day-long battle that was only won after a heavy concentration of field and medium artillery neutralized the defenders allowing the Black Watch and Fort Garries to close with the enemy.

The Black Watch, under their new commanding officer, Lieutenant-Colonel Syd Thompson, liberated Holten in a well-executed infantry-tank advance. Once in town the snipers and jubilant civilians made mopping-up operations especially difficult but the battalion was able to clear Holten and the forested area to the north known as the

Soldiers from the Royal Highland Light Infantry aboard "Kangaroo" armoured personnel carriers near Groningen.
LAC PA 130937

Holtenberg which was to become the site of the last Canadian Military Cemetery in Europe.

On the night of 7-8 April, two Special Air Service units, the 2nd and 3rd Régiments de Chasseurs Parachutistes, were dropped into northern Holland to prevent bridge demolition and seize two airfields near Steenwijk. Operation "Amherst" was a costly and largely unnecessary intervention carried out because of pressure to use these elite troops before the war ended. One group of 16 SAS officers and men fought a fierce engagement at Westerbork where the SS operated a transit camp used to hold Dutch Jews before they were deported to the death camps in Poland. Anne Frank and her family, captured in August 1944, were at Kamp Westerbork before they were sent east to be murdered at Auschwitz and Bergen-Belsen. On 12 April 1945 patrols from 8 Recce Regiment and elements of the South Saskatchewan Regiment reached the camp ensuring the safety of the 876 prisoners who had escaped the deportations.

Second Division continued north towards Groningen reaching the outskirts of the city on 13 April. Major-General Bruce Matthews had no reason to anticipate a major battle for the city as the enemy seemed to be fleeing east into Germany as fast as possible. Groningen, the largest centre in Northern Holland, was however an outer bastion of the fortified zone protecting the Ems estuary and the German North Sea port of Emden. The inner city was encircled by canals and with the bridges blown and the main routes blocked by anti-tank obstacles Groningen would not be difficult to defend if the garrison of some 7,000 men could be effectively organized.

The liberation of Groningen began when the vanguard of 4th Brigade, a company of infantry from the RHLI with a Fort Garry Horse squadron, a troop of self-propelled guns from 2nd Anti-Tank Regiment and a Toronto Scottish machine gun platoon overwhelmed an enemy blocking force and captured 250 prisoners. This success encouraged aggressive action but the Rileys quickly discovered that the main German defences could not be easily breached. The lead Fort Garry tank was destroyed and all attempts to penetrate the city were fiercely resisted. Brigadier Cabeldu committed both the Essex Scottish and Royal Regiments to what was becoming a house-to-house battle.

By the afternoon of day 2 (14 April) 4th Brigade had secured the railway yards and train station but the ring canal defences were still intact. A Tor Scot machine gun section installed on the roof of the railway station provided covering fire but even with Kangaroos the Essex could not break into the inner city.

Matthews decided to send 5th Brigade into Groningen from the west hoping to outflank the enemy defences. All three battalions were able to

Above: A Canadian convoy passes through the peaceful streets of Winschoten, Netherlands.
CFJIC ZK 991-1

Below: Lance Corporal E.R. Beattie directs traffic in Winschoten.
CFJIC ZK 992

Top: A Dutch soldier and a Canadian soldier talk with a local farmer and his family. CFJIC ZK 990-2

Above: A Dutch soldier, a farmer and a Canadian soldier in a field of wild cabbage ordered grown by the Germans for the oil found in the seeds. CFJIC ZK 990-1

Right: Private A. Longuepee talks to a young Dutch girl, Winschoten, Netherlands. CFJIC ZK 993

Soldiers from the Lake Superior Regiment marching through Almelo, Netherlands, 5 April 1945.
LAC PA 116098

Men from the 4th Canadian Infantry Division in Sögel, Germany, 10 April 1945.
LAC PA 129754

reach the canal but their advance was slowed by determined enemy machine gun and light flak guns firing 20 mm shells. Day 3 of the battle began early on a cool Sunday morning. Cabeldu's 4th Brigade was withdrawn and 6th Brigade took over the southern perimeter. Brigadier J.V. Allard orchestrated a well-supported attack employing much of the divisional artillery. By mid-morning the lead elements of both brigades were across the canal and clearing the city street by street. The standard method was to knock on a door and ask if there were any Germans around. The South Sasks reached the Vismarkt by 1330 hours but it took three more hours to reach the nearby Grote Markt which was strongly defended. That evening, loudspeakers delivered a poignant message: "It is senseless to destroy the city any further. A large Canadian army is approaching from the southwest. Surrender. If you come with your hands up and walk south nothing will happen to you."

Fifth Brigade may not have been a large Canadian army but all three battalions were advancing steadily, threatening the enemy's escape route. By dawn on 16 April most the German forces had withdrawn to the northeast corner of the city and were intent on reaching Delfzijl. The garrison commander surrendered Groningen to the commanding officer of the FMRs, Lieutenant-Colonel J.A. Dextraze, shortly after mid-day but fighting continued throughout the afternoon.

The Canadians suffered 209 casualties in Groningen including 43 men killed in action. More than 5,000 German troops became prisoners of war. Tragically, 110 civilians lost their lives in the battle and more than 250 buildings were destroyed or extensively damaged. The soldiers who fought this difficult battle could be forgiven for thinking their war might be over but on 19 April, 2nd Division was ordered into Germany to support Montgomery's battle for Bremen.

4th Division

Delden, Sögel and the Küsten Canal

It was at the Twente Canal that 4th Armoured Division hit its first serious opposition. Major-General Vokes ordered Brigadier Moncel to use "Tiger Force" at a crossing point near Delden. The Lincs, with supporting and diversionary fire from the Lake Superiors and Governor General's

Foot Guards, were over the canal quickly enough, but before long the bridgehead was heavily counterattacked and one company was completely cut off. The company commander, Major J.A. Dunlop, called mortars down on his own position to defeat one attack and preserved a foothold. Early on the morning of 4 April the Lincs moved into Delden where the town's citizens went wild with joy and relief. The Twente Canal and Delden may seem like minor affairs compared to the Hochwald but the Lincs alone took 67 casualties in the day's fighting.

The advance of 4th Division from the Twente Canal was made considerably easier when the 1st Polish Armoured Division was added to General Simonds' order of battle and directed towards Leer. This left 4th Division with a fairly narrow zone of operations along the axis Almelo-Meppen-Sögel-Oldenburg. Monty wished to transfer control of 4th Division to 30th British Corps as its key role was flank protection for the British thrust to Bremen, but Crerar politely declined. The five-division Canadian Army was at last together and Crerar preferred to keep it that way.

The approach to Oldenburg was not without serious incidents, including the battle fought by the Lake Superior Regiment in the streets of Sögel where a German counterattack force included numbers of young men in no discernable military uniforms. One of the units caught up in the fighting at Sögel was 12 Canadian Field Ambulance. The unit's war diary records the following: "They [the enemy] pressed an attack of approx. 30 men right down the street on which we were situated. Our men had to take up arms. Some of the enemy were killed within ten yards of the Advanced Dressing Station entrance." The soldiers' attitudes towards the enemy hardened in these affairs and mortars, artillery and, when available, tactical air power, were used without any of the restraint evident in the Netherlands. The worst reprisal incident occurred in Friesoythe when rumours that the death of Lieutenant-Colonel Wigle, CO of the Argylls, had been caused by a sniper in civilian clothes led to setting the town on fire.

On 16 April the division was confronted with the task of an assault crossing of the Küsten Canal, a water barrier more than 100 feet wide, that seemed to be well defended. For 4th Division this meant a long and costly battle. The Algonquins, with memories of the Leopold and other canals in their minds, established a bridgehead and were then joined by the Argylls. All through the 18th counterattacks beat against the perimeter. By the morning of the 19th the exhausted, but determined, engineers had a bridge in place and a squadron of BCR tanks sped across to provide sorely needed assistance. When the battered enemy withdrew the division regrouped for a final push into Northern Germany.

German children surrender near Sögel, Germany, 10 April 1945. In Holland the civilians greeted the soldiers with flags and flowers, but in Germany any male of almost any age could be a soldier. These children have the look of "scared kids," not "teenage fanatics" but they have been told to turn out their pockets and raise their hands.
LAC PA 113697

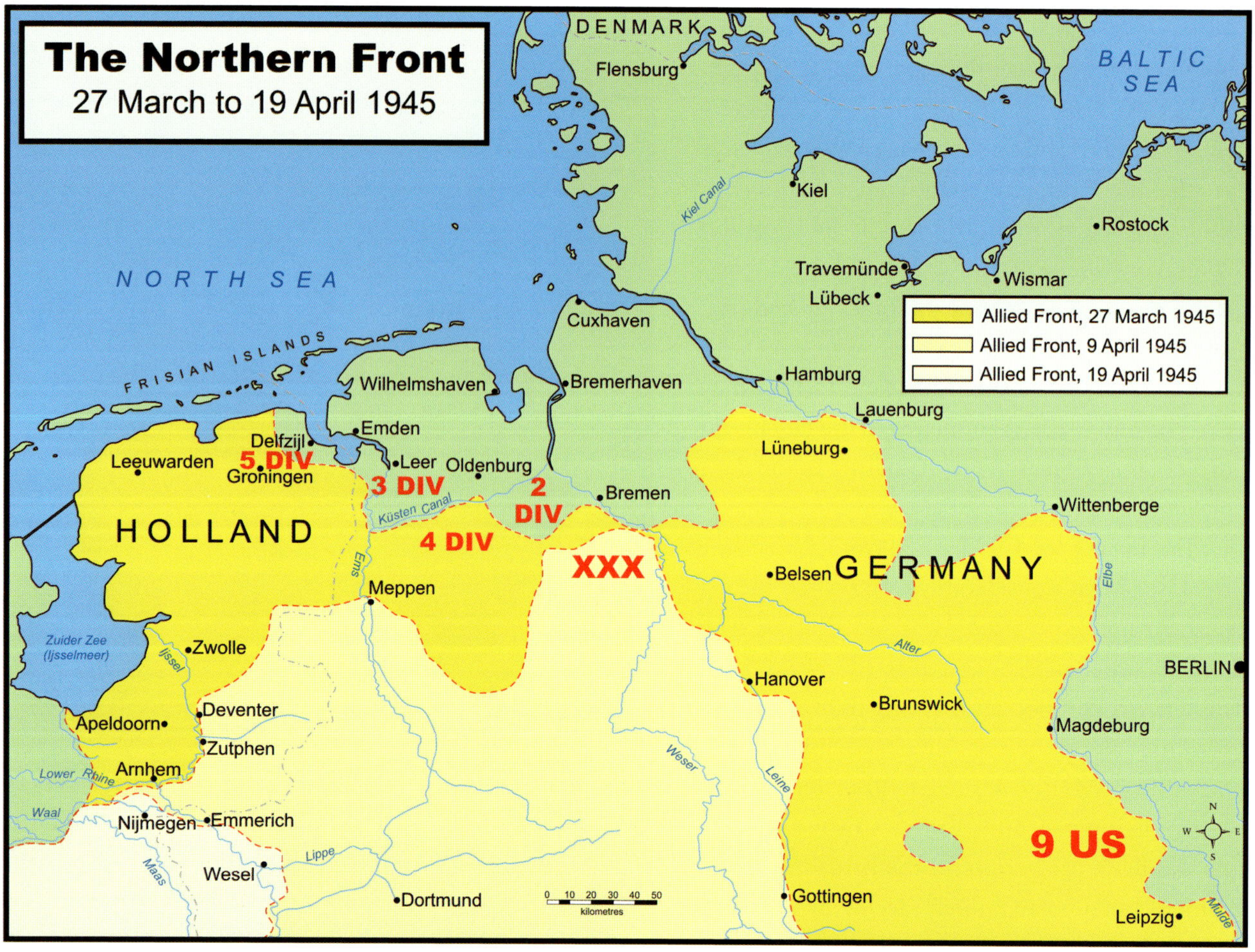

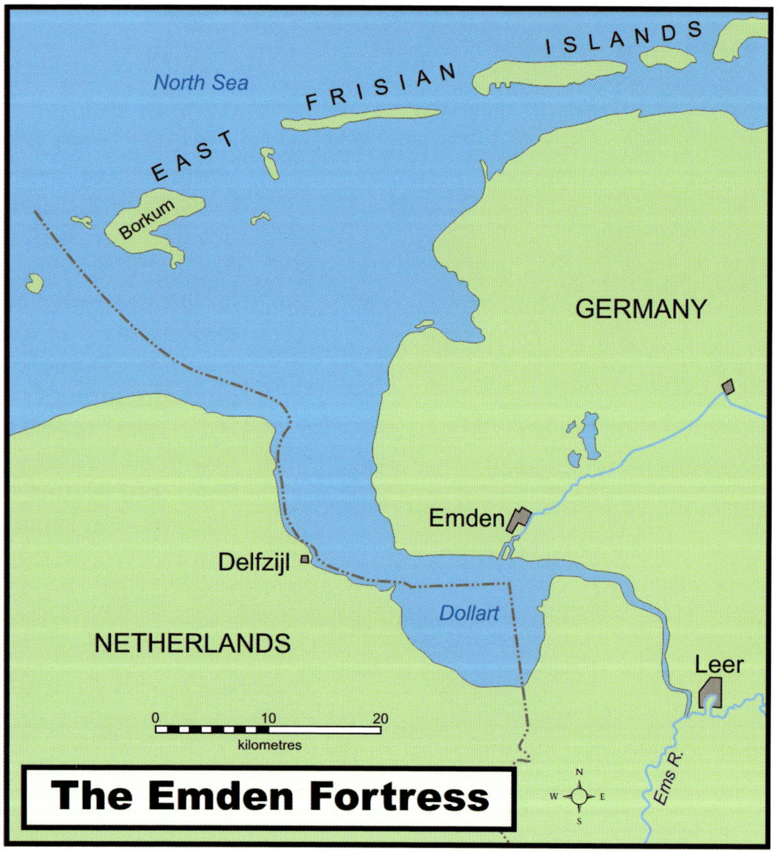

"East Meets West" – A Soviet soldier shakes hands with an American G.I., Torgau, Germany, 27 April 1945.
LAC PA 146288

The Last Battles

Delfzijl, Leer, Bad Zwischenahn, Oldenburg and Wismar

The loss of young lives is always tragic, but death on the battlefield in the last days of a war seems especially hard. Before we examine the events of late April and early May it is important to understand the context within which these terrible engagements were fought.

After the successful Rhine crossings there could be no doubt that the end of the war was weeks, rather than months, away. Newspaper headlines and BBC broadcasts trumpeted Allied victories and offered predictions of how long it would take to reach Berlin. The death of Franklin Delano Roosevelt, the US president, on 12 April shocked the western world. On the same day Ninth US Army reached the Elbe, 57 miles west of Berlin. Two days later Eisenhower ordered Ninth Army to halt as the Soviet Army launched its major offensive against Berlin. Ike was unwilling to risk American lives in a battle for territory well within the Soviet occupation zone. The decision to stop Ninth Army in the Berlin sector did not mean that the other American armies ceased operations. Fighting continued in Bavaria and Czechoslovakia until the final hours of the war ensuring that the Nazis did not establish a final bastion in the south.

To the north, 21st Army Group was required to develop major offensive operations in late April. Eisenhower would not try and take Berlin without political direction from London and Washington but he was determined to cross the Elbe River in the north and drive to the coast of the Baltic Sea, sealing off the Danish peninsula from the Red Army. To assist Montgomery, Ike provided the 18th US Airborne Corps, which included 6th British Airborne Division and thus 1st Canadian Parachute Battalion. This Corps struck out for Wismar on the Baltic Coast while Monty's three

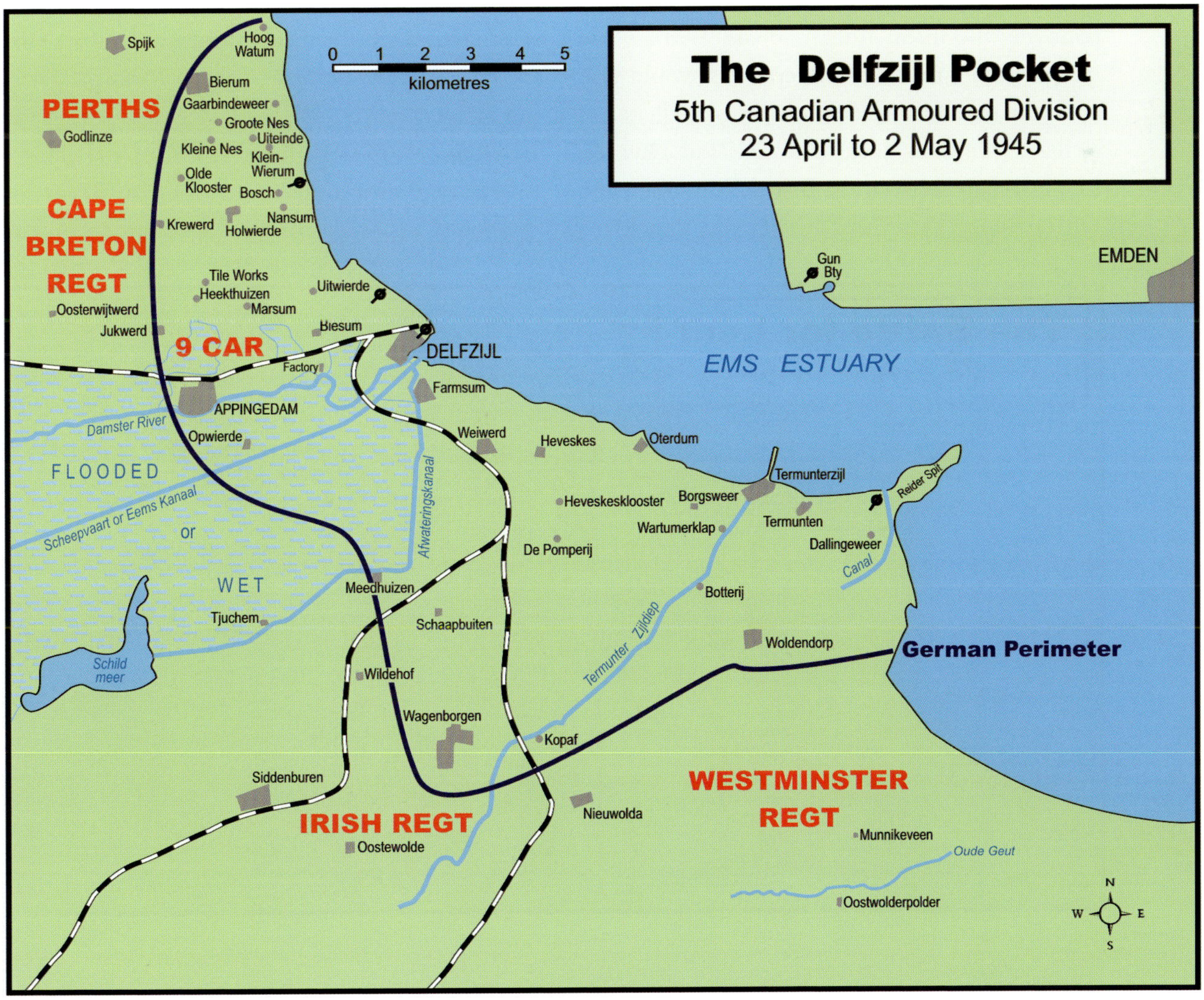

British Corps attacked north completing the destruction of the German forces and establishing control of Hamburg, the Kiel Canal and the province of Schleswig-Holstein.

Another and perhaps equally important reason for pressing offensive operations to the end was also related to the Soviet Union. In the last weeks of the war the western Allies were repeatedly approached with offers to surrender German units in the west while fighting continued on the Russian front. The Allies, still hopeful that post-war cooperation with the Soviets was possible, were determined to avoid any suggestion that they were easing up on the Germans allowing troops to be shifted to fight the Red Army. The consequence was that, except in Ninth Army's sector, the American, British, Canadian, French and Polish Units were in action until the end.

Second Canadian Corps' particular task was to clear the Emden-Wilhelmshaven peninsula. These operations would give the Allies control of the north German ports, with the added bonus of removing the threat from U-boats, E-boats and midget submarines. The operations would also open the harbours needed to supply soldiers and civilians. Simonds decided to use 2nd Division to fill the gap between the British at Bremen and 4th Division. Then 3rd Division was transferred to Germany to begin operations directed at Leer and Emden. This shift meant that 5th Armoured Division had to take over the advance on Delfzijl, the Dutch town across the estuary from Emden. Delfzijl was an important port in its own right and was needed for the anticipated effort to liberate the Frisian Islands.

Major-General Hoffmeister inherited responsibility for the northwest Netherlands on 23 April. Delfzijl and its guns were part of the defences of Emden and the Ems estuary so the port could not be simply isolated until the war ended. It was, however, a Dutch city so neither heavy nor medium bombers could be used and Hoffmeister was determined to limit the use of medium and heavy artillery to minimize civilian casualties. He consulted his combat leaders including NCOs before imposing to this restriction.

Since the enemy possessed abundant ammunition for the heavy coastal guns, night attacks were planned to limit casualties to the Canadians and the eight Netherlands Independent Companies who helped to liberate Delfzijl. The operation, code-named "Canada," was primarily an infantry battle. The Perth Regiment began the reduction of the perimeter capturing the villages of Krewerd and Holwierde. The Irish Regiment launched an attack from Wagenborgen on the

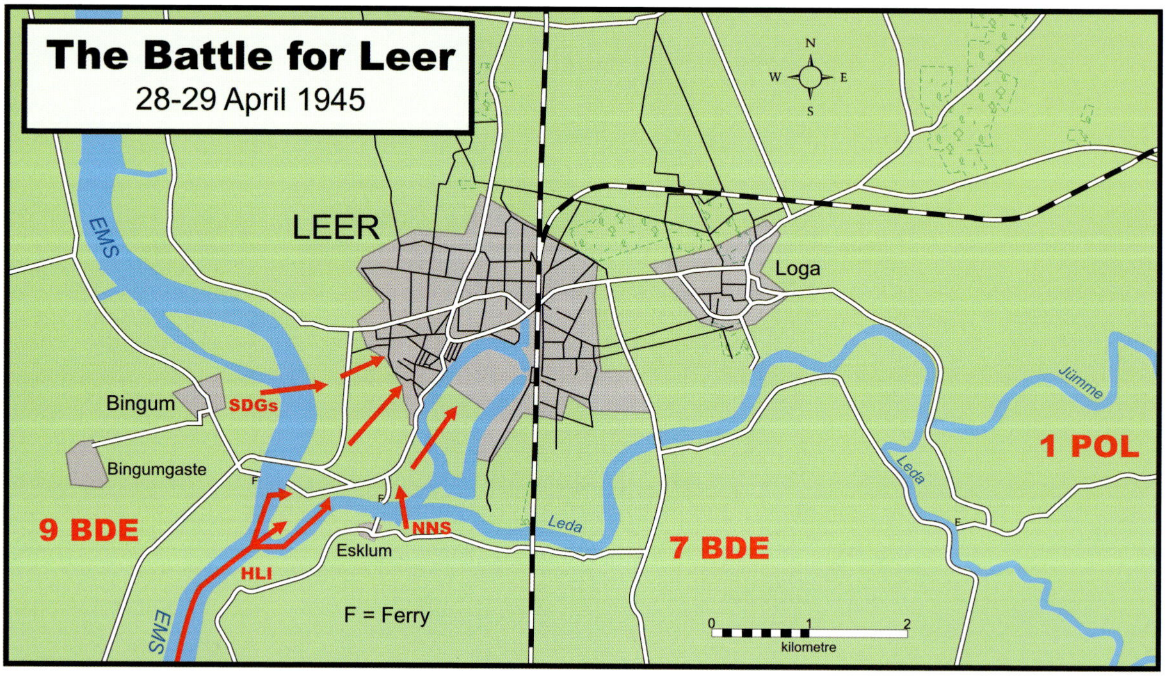

25th and the next day the Westminster Regiment (Motor) started north to capture the eastern gun batteries.

Brigadier I.S. Johnston, commander of 11th Brigade, had been told to co-ordinate the capture of Delfzijl with 3rd Division's attack on Emden. In the event 3rd Division was heavily engaged at Leer. Johnston decided that finishing off German resistance quickly would be less costly than a slow advance under punishing artillery fire. By the evening of 30 April the Brigade reached the inner defensive perimeter. The Cape Breton Highlanders attacked that night but minefields slowed the advance. Tanks of the New Brunswick Hussars were sent to help and the battlegroup fought its way into the town. The Irish Regiment, with a squadron of Hussars' tanks completed the capture of the eastern part of the fortress the same day. The garrison commander surrendered officially that evening, 2 May. More than 4,000 prisoners were taken in the ten-day battle that marked the end of the war for 5th Armoured Division.

The "Water Rats" of 3rd Division faced a most difficult, if all too familiar task – an assault crossing of a wide river estuary. The objective was Leer, a port and communication centre with good roads to Emden and Wilhelmshaven. Operation "Duck" began with the North Nova Scotia Highlanders using storm-boats to cross the Leda River and seize a bridgehead, while the Highland Light Infantry sailed up the River Ems to land at Leerort. The Sherbrooke Fusiliers, with 6th Anti-Tank Regiment and the two Royal Canadian Engineers Field Companies, were added to an order of battle which included "Crocodiles," heavy artillery and Typhoons from 84 Group.

The attack achieved tactical surprise and both assault battalions were quickly on their objectives. Tragically, part of the reserve battalion, the Glens, was caught in heavy machine gun fire which sank two boats in the second wave. The battle for Leer developed into a series of isolated street battles and by the evening of 29 April the town was secure. Seventh Brigade started towards Emden handing over the lead to 8th Brigade on 3 May.

Top: Infantry of Les Fusiliers Mont-Royal taking cover between two Churchill tanks during an attack near Oldenburg, Germany, 29 April 1945
LAC PA 137471

Above: Royal Regiment of Canada infantry supported by Fort Garry Horse tanks advance from Hatten to Dingstede, 24 April 1945 LAC PA 143675

Left: Officers of the 1st Canadian Parachute Battalion enjoy a quiet moment. Greven, Germany, 4 April 1945.
LAC PA 115016

The next day, as negotiations for the surrender of Aurich were underway, the order came to cease all operations. A campaign which had begun for the division on the beaches of Normandy was finally over.

* * * * *

The fighting in the Küsten Canal bridgehead was among the most difficult 4th Division encountered in the war. When German counterattacks ceased on 22 April the infantry battalions had suffered more than 200 casualties. The push north turned out to be equally difficult. The infantry fought a draining battle for Edewecht which lasted until the 25th. The terrain was boggy and flat with forest plantations. There was heavy fighting for Ekern before the final push into Bad Zwischenahn. The resort town was surrounded on 1 May and the Burgomeister "was invited to choose between unconditional surrender and annihilation." He persuaded the remaining garrison to agree to surrender. The advance continued until 3 May with 1st Canadian Armoured Car Regiment (The Royal Canadian Dragoons) and the Manitoba Dragoons in the lead. Major-General Vokes also employed the First Hussars and the 1st Belgian SAS Regiment to cover the left flank and maintain contact with the Polish Armoured Division.

Second Division began the advance from Ahlhorn to Oldenburg on 19 April. At first there was little opposition but at Kirchhatten a battlegroup made up of NCO trainees had dug-in, determined to hold the village. The Queen's Own Cameron Highlanders had to face a serious counterattack which Canadian tanks and artillery quickly crushed. There were similar fire-fights on 4th Brigade's axis while to the east 5th Brigade suffered from continuous mortaring in the capture of Delmenhorst. The Black Watch, who had fought the Brigade's first battle at Caen, led off in the last engagement at Hude. Enemy resistance slackened on 2 May and the next day 4th and 6th Brigades entered Oldenburg which enemy troops had abandoned

* * * * *

The last few days of the war in Germany were a miserable period for everyone involved. It rained steadily and the tired and wet bedraggled men were asked to maintain pressure without taking too many chances. When rotated out of action they collapsed into deep sleep. German resistance was not well organized but there seemed

Below left: Dutch civilians loading a Canadian-supplied truck with food, following an agreement between the Germans, Dutch and Allies to allow food distribution to the Dutch population. Near Wageningen, Netherlands, 3 May 1945
LAC PA 134417

Below right: A convoy of trucks filled with Allied foodstuffs being moved to German-occupied territory in the Western Netherlands, 3 May 1945
LAC PA 134418

Gunners of the 12th Field Regiment, Royal Canadian Artillery, read the victory issue of *The Maple Leaf*, Aurich, Germany, 20 May 1945
LAC PA 150931

to be no shortage of mortar rounds and a small but steady stream of casualties were evacuated.

With four Canadian divisions committed to action, the last two weeks of the war produced a large number of casualties, including 490 fatalities. Of these, 114 died in May, including 12 on the last day of the war in Europe. Continuing the advance into northern Germany while the Soviets were in the suburbs of Berlin made little military sense, but the Allies had promised to maintain pressure to prevent the transfer of German units to the east and Montgomery's orders reflected this commitment.

One last major task remained, the advance to the Baltic to safeguard Denmark. Eisenhower wanted priority for this operation, a request that prompted a last bitter protest from Montgomery, who replied that if the Russians reached Denmark it would be because of Eisenhower's faulty strategy. Montgomery might ignore Eisenhower but when Churchill demanded action, the Field Marshal moved promptly, advancing the date of the dash

The evacuation of German troops from Holland over the Zuider Zee, May 1945.
CFJIC ZK 1002

to the Baltic. This operation was carried out by the 18th US Airborne Corps with 6th British Airborne Division under command. Since Brigadier James Hill's 3rd Parachute Brigade was in the vanguard there was no hesitation and when 1st Canadian Parachute Battalion linked up with the Scots Greys of the Royal Armoured Corps they discovered that tanks could go quite fast even with paratroops clinging onto them.

Hill decided to continue north without pause and the columns raced by thousands of armed German soldiers who, along with masses of civilians, were fleeing from the Russians. The Canadians were in the lead when the Baltic was reached and it fell to Lieutenant-Colonel Fraser Eadie and his men to confront Soviet forces on the outskirts of Wismar. A fine mixture of determination and diplomacy was required to convince the Soviets that Wismar was going to stay in Canadian hands but the tough, experienced paratroopers were the right men for the job. Captain Richard Hilborn, who had jumped into France on D-Day, took on the liaison role with the Russians and managed to smooth over differences with the aid of a generous supply of champagne.

On the morning of 5 May 1945 messages ordering all units to cease offensive operations were issued and the news spread quickly. There were few signs of celebration. The predominant emotion was simple relief at having survived. As they waited to return to Canada the men and women of Canada's armed forces had ample time to reflect on their experience. The letters and diaries of the period express pride in their achievements, a determination to remember fallen comrades and hope for a better way of living in a world without war.

The Tour

The wide dispersal of Canadian units across northern Holland and Germany presents a real challenge in planning a brief tour. The following suggestions are based on our visits to the area but we have not covered all possibilities. Many visitors will wish to end their trip in Amsterdam so we suggest exploring the north-east before travelling to Apeldoorn and Amsterdam. The roads in the Netherlands are well marked but you will need a good road map. Once in the Netherlands you can purchase 1:150,000 *toeristenkart* maps that will allow you to find the smallest village.

Doetinchem, with a memorial to the Fort Garry Horse, is just 30 minutes from Arnhem or the Rhine crossings west of Emmerich. Zutphen and the western end of the Twente Canal are less than an hour north on the N317. The Germans tried to defend both the city and the Twente Canal line but the Royal Regiment of Canada rushed

2nd Canadian Infantry Division's crossing site over the Twente Canal. The north side of the canal is to the right.

Left: Tree near the railway line from Zutphen to Winterswijk planted by inhabitants of the neighbourhood of Warken in honour of their Canadian liberators.

Far left: The plaque near the tree states: "Resting place Maple Leaf. This tree was planted by inhabitants of the neighbourhood of Warken to commemorate the liberation of the neighbourhood on Monday 2 April 1945. The neighbourhood honours the liberators of the Canadian Essex Scottish Regiment and those fallen during the period 1940 - 1945." Photos by Evert Stieber

the canal near the village of Almen and together with the Rileys beat off counterattacks "by dirty, grubby, slender youths, boys and old men."

Third Division used the Almen bridgehead to envelope Zutphen from the east while 9th Brigade fought its way forward into the town from the south. The battle for Zutphen had to be completed quickly because 1st Canadian Division was to begin the advance into western Holland. Unfortunately, Zutphen was strongly-defended. Eighth Brigade undertook the final advance into the city and it required hand-to-hand and house-to-house fighting. Crocodile flame-throwing tanks persuaded the last holdouts to flee across the river. Zutphen is a quiet provincial city with a well-preserved town centre. The cathedral, damaged in 1945, has been rebuilt and the nearby town hall allows the visitor to see the river and much of the city. There is a memorial east of the city on the grounds of the hospital. The Rev. Hank Dykman, a Dutch-born resident of Guelph, Ontario, has assisted in the creation of this monument for 31 Canadians and one Englishman who died liberating the Zutphen area in April 1945.

Continue north on the N48. Just before the village of Gorssel turn left towards the river. When you reach the banks of the Ijssel you are at the forming up point for 1st Division's Operation "Cannonshot." There was some resistance on the west bank but after the Princess Patricia's Canadian Light Infantry captured Wilp the advance to the Apeldoorn Canal went quickly. There are small cairns commemorating the crossing on both sides of the river.

Drive north on the N48 to the Schipbeek Canal south of Deventer. The main attack on the city came from the east through the village of Schalkhaar. There is a market in the main square on Fridays and Saturdays and some fine public buildings as well as sidewalk cafés. Boat trips on the Ijssel may also be of interest to you.

From Deventer the Canadian visitor should drive east on the A1 or N344 to Holten and the forested Holterberg area where the Canadian Military Cemetery is located. The Commonwealth War Graves Commission Cemetery signs are not evident until you get close to the site. Go north on the main street "Dorpstraat" following signs for Holterberg. The "Molenbelterweg" road leads to the "de Holterberg" road and then signs will guide you along a dirt road to a place of extraordinary calmness and beauty. The decision to bury those

Holten Canadian War Cemetery

Above: From the air. (Photo by Evert Stieber)

Left: As is appears today.

Below: As it appeared shortly after the war. (CFJIC ZK 1129-2)

Bottom: Christmas Eve candlelight ceremony. (Photo by Evert Stieber)

killed in Northern Holland and Germany at a cemetery in the Holtenberg was made by Simonds because the pine woods reminded him of Canada. Soldiers awaiting repatriation did much of the preparatory work and by the summer of 1946 the 1,496 graves were in place. The Dutch authorities gave 14 acres to Canada and the front part of the cemetery was laid out as a large heather garden. Every year on 4 May a service of remembrance is held here and on Christmas Eve school children place a lighted candle at each grave. No Canadian visiting the Netherlands should miss this extraordinary place.

From Holten you may wish to drive east to Delden where 4th Armoured Division crossed the Twente Canal. From Holten we suggest you follow 2nd Division's route to Ommen and Groningen. At Ommen, which the Black Watch liberated, there is a plaque on a townhouse near the river. Groningen was defended by a determined enemy and required the entire resources of Second Division. You can examine the area near the railway station where 4th Brigade fought, and then walk into town via the two main squares to get some sense of the challenges presented by this urban battlefield. Our website provides further information.

There is a plaque on the town hall (Stadhuis) with an inscription which commemorates "The liberation of Groningen by Canadian Armed Forces April 1945." The city started a "Liberation Forest" of 33,000 Maple trees for the 50th anniversary <www.groningen.nl>. The Canadian Allied Forces Museum in Groningen opened to the public in May 2010. It features many restored vehicles and an Avro Anson aircraft. <www.canadianalliedforces.com>

Delfzijl is a brief drive north through striking polder country. The town was badly damaged during the war and has been extensively rebuilt. There is a memorial to the resistance in the area, a silver swan which symbolizes the code-name of the local resistance group. The individual villages on the Delfzijl perimeter may readily be visited but it is unlikely that a 5th Division veteran would recognize very much.

If you wish to visit the battlefields of northern Germany take the N362 south to the A7. The Küsten Canal crossing which forced 4th Division into a protracted and bloody battle is located just to the east of the Friesoythe-Bad Zwischenahn road. Take the N72 south from the A7/E22 and follow the signs to Friesoythe then north to the canal. From here you can visit most of the towns and villages which were the focal points of German resistance but it is not easy to reconstruct a visual picture of the events of 1945.

Return to Groningen. Third Division's advance may be traced in reverse by driving west to Leeuwarden. The Frisian Resistance Museum emphasises the local struggle though there is reference to the liberation.

Your next stop should be Apeldoorn, a city of considerable interest, famous for the Het Loo Palace and gardens. The Royal Canadian Regiment, working with the First Hussars, made the initial advance on 15 April along the Deventerstraat but were stopped at the Apeldoorn Canal which was well-defended. Plans were made to clear the city using a minimum of artillery but the rapid advance of 5th Armoured Division and 2nd Brigade south and west of the city persuaded the enemy to abandon Apeldoorn. The population, doubly grateful for a liberation without the destruction of their city reached out to embrace the Canadians.

Every five years since 1985 Apeldoorn has been the scene of some extraordinary anniversary commemorations. The Veterans Parade from the Het Loo Palace brought most of the city into the streets "waving more Maple Leaf flags then could be seen at any parade in Canada." From Apeldoorn it is an easy drive to Amsterdam through you should be aware that morning traffic (especially Mondays) into the city frequently creates gridlock. There are restrictions on automobiles in the city centre so be sure your hotel has parking. If you are returning home via Amsterdam's airport, Schipol, the route is well marked.

◇◇◇◇◇◇◇◇◇◇◇◇◇◇◇◇

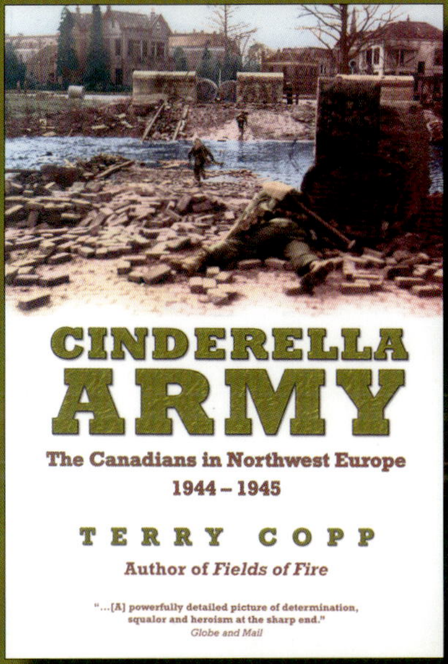

Cinderella Army: The Canadians in Northwest Europe, 1944-1945

By Terry Copp

University of Toronto Press, 2006
ISBN 9780802039255 cloth
Published Sep 2006
ISBN 9780802095220 paper
Published Oct 2007

In his controversial and award-winning 2003 book *Fields of Fire*, Terry Copp offered a stunning reversal of accepted military history, challenging the conventional view that the Canadian contribution to the Battle of Normandy was a failure. *Cinderella Army* continues the story of the operations carried out by the First Canadian Army in the last nine months of the war, and extends the argument developed in *Fields of Fire* that "the achievement of the Allied and especially the Canadian armies... has been greatly underrated while the effectiveness of the German army has been greatly exaggerated." Copp supports this argument with research conducted on numerous trips to the battlefields of France, Belgium, Holland and Germany. His detailed knowledge of the battlefield terrain, along with contemporary maps and air photos, allows Copp to explore the defensive positions that Canadian soldiers were required to overcome, and to illustrate how impressive their achievements truly were.

Except for a brief period during the Rhineland battle, the First Canadian Army was the smallest to serve under Eisenhower's command. The Canadian component of that Army never totalled more that 185,000 of the four million Allied troops serving in Northwest Europe. It is, however, evident that the divisions of 2nd Canadian Corps played a role disproportionate to their numbers. Their contribution to operations designed to secure the Channel Ports and open the approaches to Antwerp together with the battles in the Rhineland place them among the most heavily committed and sorely tried divisions in the Allied armies. By the end of 1944 3rd Canadian Division had suffered the highest number of casualties in 21 Army Group with 2nd Canadian Division ranking a close second. Among armoured divisions, 4th Canadian was at the top of the list as was 2nd Canadian Armoured Brigade among the independent tank brigades. Overall Canadian casualties were twenty percent higher than in comparable British formations. This was a direct result of the much greater number of days that Canadian units were involved in close combat.

As passionately written and compellingly argued as its precursor, *Cinderella Army* is both an important bookend to Copp's earlier work, and stands on its own as a significant contribution to Canadian military history.

Also available from
The Laurier Centre for Military Strategic and Disarmament Studies

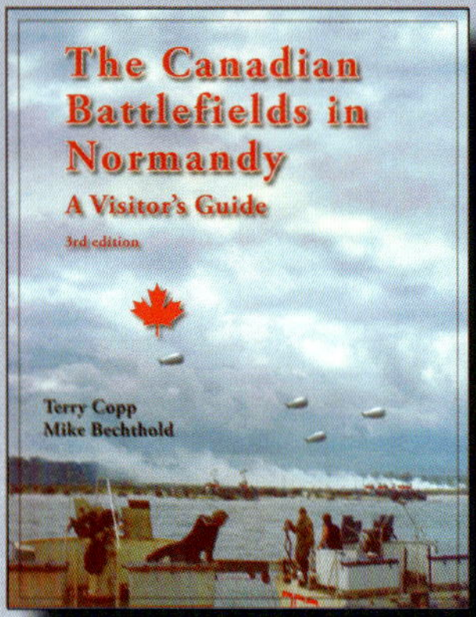

The Canadian Battlefields in Normandy: A Visitor's Guide, 3rd ed.

Terry Copp and Mike Bechthold
128 pages, ISBN13: 978-0-97834-414-6

A revised edition of the bestselling guidebook by one of Canada's foremost military historians brings the Normandy campaign to life with never-before-seen full-colour photographs. Revised full-colour maps and updated text transport the reader back to the summer of 1944. This guide is essential reading for any Canadian who is contemplating a trip to France.

The Canadian Battlefields in Italy: Sicily and Southern Italy

Eric McGeer, Terry Copp, and Matt Symes
85 pages, ISBN13: 978-0-97834-415-3

This book transports the reader to Sicily, where Canadian soldiers fought in the summer of 1943. With remarkable new three-dimensional satellite maps, this book is sure to be enjoyable reading for anyone with an interest in Canada's Second World War experience.

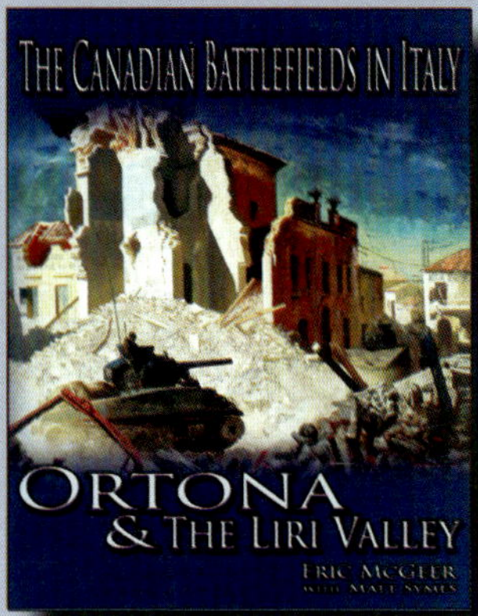

The Canadian Battlefields in Italy: Ortona and the Liri Valley

Eric McGeer, and Matt Symes
112 pages, ISBN13: 978-0-97834-410-8

The Canadian battlefields in Italy are portrayed in revolutionary, new, three-dimensional satellite maps that show the terrain and towns as they have never been seen before. The detailed narrative takes the reader through some of the toughest fighting of the Second World War.

The Canadian Battlefields in Italy: The Gothic Line and the Battle of the Rivers

Eric McGeer, and Matt Symes
158 pages, ISBN13: 978-1-92680-407-1

The third of the LCMSDS battlefield guides to concentrate on the Canadian forces in Italy, The Canadian Battlefields in Italy: The Gothic Line and the Battle of the Rivers continues the journey through the Gothic Line, Canada's greatest battle of the Italian Campaign, and on to Ravenna, where Canadian soldiers fought doggedly against the enemy and the elements in a remote corner of the war.

All titles are available at your local bookstore, or from Wilfrid Laurier University Press:
http://www.wlupress.wlu.ca/press/Series/lcmsds.shtml